S0-IWW-497

STUDIES IN AFRICAN AMERICAN HISTORY AND CULTURE

edited by

GRAHAM HODGES
COLGATE UNIVERSITY

A GARLAND SERIES

31607479
.b24268239
/3763

SAMUEL RINGGOLD WARD

Christian Abolitionist

E
449
W27
B87
1995

RONALD K. BURKE

LB 6/26/95

GARLAND PUBLISHING, Inc.
New York & London / 1995

WITHDRAWN
OHIO UNIVERSITY
LIBRARY

Copyright © 1995 Ronald K. Burke
All rights reserved

Library of Congress Cataloging-in-Publication Data

Burke, Ronald K.
Samuel Ringgold Ward, Christian abolitionist / Ronald K. Burke.
p. cm. — (Studies in African-American history and culture)
Includes bibliographical references and index.
ISBN 0-8153-1930-4 (alk. paper)
1. Ward, Samuel Ringgold, b. 1817. 2. Abolitionists—United States—Biography. 3. Afro-Americans—Biography. 4. Antislavery movements—United States. 5. Slavery and the church—United States. I. Title. II. Series.
E449.W27B87 1995
326'.092—dc20 94-42751
[B] CIP

Printed on acid-free, 250-year-life paper
Manufactured in the United States of America

Contents

Preface

In the introduction to Earl Ofari's book on Henry Highland Garnet entitled *Let Your Motto Be Resistance* he expressed disappointment that not enough definitive works were available on individuals such as Charles Langston, Frances Ellen Watkins, Sam R. Ward, Alexander Crummell, Robert Campbell, Bishop Holly, J.W. Loguen, Mammy Pleasant and other eminent African American activists. This study of the Reverend Mister Samuel Ringgold Ward is an effort to help change that condition of which Ofari is concerned.

I am grateful to several individuals for helping this study of Samuel R. Ward become a reality. I am especially indebted to Doctor Otey M. Scruggs for his invaluable knowledge of the African American experience and his many perceptive suggestions. Also, I am indebted to Doctor Paul E. Ried for assistance on style and the recommendations on content in the rhetorical analysis section of this work. I am thankful to Professor Roland E. Wolseley and Doctors D.B. Robertson and James B. Wiggins for reading the manuscript and offering suggestions for improvement. Thanks to Irwin Mallin for help in the software programming.

I wish particularly to give very special thanks to Mrs. Richard N. Wright of the Onondaga Historical Society for the newspaper clippings containing information on Ward and for her suggestion to inquire at the American Antiquarian Society in Worcester, Massachusetts for copies of Ward's newspaper, *The Impartial Citizen*. Others who aided me in my research are: F.S. Facer, Wayne County Historian, Lyons, New York; Clifton Johnson of the Amistad Research Center at Dillard University; Jacqueline Welds and Althea Silvera of the West Indes Reference Library, Institute of Jamaica; and the Jamaican Government Archivists in Spanish Town, Jamaica.

I would like to thank the helpful staffs at the following libraries: Interlibrary Loan, Bird Library, Syracuse University; Boston Public Library; Hampton Institute; University of Rochester Library; Douglas Library, Queens University, Kingston, Ontario; Department of Rare Books and Special Collections, University of Michigan; American Antiquarian Society, Worcester, Massachusetts; and the Library staff at the University of Pennsylvania.

R.K.B.

Samuel Ringgold Ward

Introduction to Part One

Charles H. Wesley argued in his article "The Negroes of New York in the Emancipation Movement," that New York in the 1820's and the 1830's "was the training ground for the rise and development of an abolition leadership."[1] When writing about the black activist Alexander Crummell Professor Otey Scruggs observed that in the just mentioned years in New York City there existed "a free black community that believed passionately in mental and moral improvement and was actively committed to the antislavery cause."[2] Further, Professor Carol George has pointed out that an all-pervasive theology in the black community stressed moral and political activism.[3] In addition, Earl Ofari has noted that: "From the 1820's on the black church occupied a dominant position in Northern black communities."[4] Having noted those scholars observations then, this study will examine one of the African Americans who participated in reform activities during those times of ferment--the Reverend Mister Samuel Ringgold Ward.

There are several biographical factors in Ward's earlier life that appear to be related to his activities as a religious reformer: he was reared by devoutly religious parents, he received his education at the religiously-oriented New York African Free-School, he found himself regularly in the presence of the leading black church activists of the day, and, as a young man he participated in church connected reform activities. These factors help explain the early formulation of Ward's doctrine of Christology.

Christology is the study of the person and works of Jesus Christ and in particular the union of Him of the divine and human natures. Two theories of Christology exist: on the one hand is the idea of the unity and distinctness of the God-man concept, while on the other is the denial of the notion of Christ as one in being with the father.[5] As a result of this difference of opinion theoreticians throughout time have developed differing viewpoints on Christology. Beginning with the Gospels (Matthew, Mark, Luke, and John) and up to and including modern times, theologians have speculated on the exact theological truth of whether or not Christ is both God and man in one. One school of thought argues that the sacred writings of the Gospel did state moreover, that historical Christ himself claimed to be both God and man. Further, Saint Paul, one of Christ's apostles and a writer of certain New Testament epistles insisted on the reality of both the Godhead and the manhood of Christ rather than to attempt to interrelate them. Another school of thought however, argues that these scriptural writings are simply the facts presented rather than an attempted explanation.

It would be inappropriate here to present a descriptive survey of Christology. Suffice it to say that the exact meaning has been a preoccupation with numerous theologians through history and three theoretical viewpoints have emerged from the continuing controversy.

Sydney Cave has characterized those views as: 1) The Patristic theory which proclaims God's victory in Christ over the devil, 2) The Penal theory which makes God's law the supreme principle to which divine love has to reconcile before man can be forgiven; and, 3) The Moral theory (sometimes known as the subjective or the exemplarist theory) which holds that the value of the death of Christ for us lies purely in the moral example which it gives us of complete love and self-sacrifice. The latter is the most intriguing and complex of all the theories and is associated with the social reformers. It asserts that our imagination is thus moved to repent, to attain holiness, and to lead a moral life. The theory has been criticized for being inadequate rather than erroneous. In short, critics claim that setting examples by living a moral life is not all that Jesus preached. That is to say, we must not lose the meaning of God's love, else we fall short of appreciating its full wonder.[6]

Samuel Ringgold Ward could be classified as an exemplarist. However it must be recognized that his doctrine of Christology embodied elements of value included in each of the above-mentioned theories. In addition to retaining a strong faith in God's ancient decrees, he put complete trust in his own willingness to serve the oppressed.

Christ impressed Ward as an extremely vivid force; His life and work were at the forefront of Ward's thought. In this study it will be shown how Ward's fervent admiration for Jesus created the motivation which involved him in social, moral, and political reform. Of Christ he said: "as God he is our Saviour--as Man he is our example." Christ, he believed constituted the true standard of moral excellence. Through His Christian works men and women can become closer to God. Ward recognized that to emulate Jesus by serving men and women exemplified life's *summum bonum.*

A compassionate man Ward made a crucial decision early in his life to follow in the footsteps of Jesus by participating in actions intended to improve the human condition. He asserted that he would carry the gospel to the "benighted portion" of humanity. At an early age he joined the ranks of the reformers. He integrated his doctrine of Christology with various forms of communication: he spoke at antislavery society meetings, he upheld the principles of those societies by holding office, he undertook antislavery speaking tours, he instructed his audiences on social and moral elevation, he edited and published antislavery newspapers, and he engaged in political activities.

Ward's interpretation of the life of Christ centered on the cross, that is, he perceived Jesus's suffering as the perfect love of one who sought nothing for himself but directed his love to all men and women. Of all the great revealers throughout time none was as unsullied as Jesus Christ who was crucified. A survey of Ward's contributions to reform will bear out that critique.

Ward perceived the malice and evil brought upon Christ as similar to the unrighteous treatment perpetrated on the black man. The author James H. Cone analyzes that viewpoint as follows:

> One has only to read the gospel to be convinced of the central importance of Jesus Christ in the Christian faith. According to the New Testament, Jesus is the man for others who view his existence as inextricably tied to other men to the degree that his own Person is inexplicable apart from others. The others, of course, refer to all men, especially the oppressed, the unwanted of society, the "sinners." He is God himself coming into the very depths of human existence for the sole purpose of striking off the chains of slavery, thereby freeing men from unGodly principalities and powers that hinder his relationship with God.[7]

Ward further believed that each one of us carries a cross which extends beyond individual patience or personal tolerance. Despite this burden, it is the responsibility of all men and women to rid the world of its evils. This God-given task teaches all of us wisdom and humility through suffering. It is not so much the cross of a martyr as it is the cross of a Christ-like person. Self-interest is to be avoided and reward for services done is unthinkable. Needless to say, the good works are helping the helpless. Ward expressed his own bearing of a cross when he said: "As a man, a Christian, especially as a black man, my labours must be antislavery labours, because mine must be an antislavery life."[8]

In Christ Ward recognized the feasibility of liberation for the African Americans, but it would not materialize by prayer alone. Oppression had to be abolished, he believed, by Christ-like labors which would be in the form of improving the social and moral conditions of the black people.

Ward had faith in Scriptural testimony that God will not tolerate acts of oppression and inevitably divine intervention will occur: "O my suffering, sighing people, there is hope for you--hope in your improvement, in your own powers; in the gathering, increasing sympathy of Europe; but, most of all, in the promises of the faithful God."[9] The white person's sins could be eradicated by each responsible person doing his or her part in the struggle for justice since the poorest of the poor are defenseless before the wicked and the powerful. Ward had faith that his people would be liberated by a "God of the oppressed." God, after all, consistently looked to the weak of the earth.

To Ward, God existed as more than an abstraction. God comprised Jesus Christ, prayer, faith, and good works. Ward noted that if Jesus spent his life among the poor then Christians too must serve the underclasses. Christians, he thought, must emulate Christ and involve themselves in lessening the misery created by the unrighteous.

Ward's doctrine did not espouse the belief held by the Second Adventists. The Adventists believed that Christ would reign in glory upon his return to the earth. They claimed that men and women must wait in anticipation for the second coming of Christ. When the second coming occurred the heavens would open up and bands of angels would sing hallelujah choruses on a glowing horizon. All would be beautiful. The Adventists believed it unimportant to labor in reforms of the day since time would cease for everyone at the Advent of Christ. What was more the Adventists claimed that at this time it would not be plausible for the existence of a righteous government. They understood that the spirit of God represented the only power in the universe able to overcome evil. Thus, participating in reform actions to the Adventist would be considered a complete waste of time. In general, the Adventists emphasized moral solutions to social problems, that is, as one religious historian so aptly put it: "They were taking refuge from the gloomy social outlook in purely spiritual contemplation."[10]

However Ward's evaluation of the Advent embodied fundamental differences. He believed that suffering would be relieved as a result of the works of Christ and man--not just Christ alone. Ward perceived the task to be not only to preach the word of God but to abolish evil by acting responsibly in social and moral reform. He looked to Christ as saying: "Occupy till I come." Ward interpreted that as instructions to "Preach and practice the truth, and the whole truth, so long as time shall last."[11] Subsequent to scrutinizing the Adventist creed Ward concluded that they were naive in their conception of the Second Coming. The Adventist should have realized that men and women cannot sit and wait for the millennial peace suddenly to occur. People must involve themselves in the "event," or become creative and willingly confront the oppressors of the world. Ward believed deeply that the realization of social and moral justice eventuates when God and Men and Women in Christ are actively engaged in improving the human condition.

Reform then, comprised the cooperative venture of God, Christ, and Men and Women in pursuit of African American liberation. When Christ ultimately reigns, His rule will take the form of emancipation of the enslaved. Just as Jesus saved men and women from death through His resurrection Ward endeavored to liberate the oppressed through his presence on earth.

Ward dedicated his life to the ideal that unselfish labors in the cause of the meek and powerless represents an expression of the highest good. To elevate his people he would practice the message of Christ: he would be a suffering servant. Devoid of any desire for material things Ward pledged to help redeem the downtrodden. He conducted his own war against sin.

More specifically, I will illustrate in this volume how Ward maintained a continuous vigil during his life to shatter three myths that were damaging to the African American: 1) the myth of African American intellectual inferiority, 2) the myth that African Americans engaged purposely in anti-social behavior, and, 3) the African Americans exhibited an insensitivity toward a spiritual life. As Ward participated in reform activities his dignified persona, his clergy status, and his command of language contradicted the negative messages communicated by detractors. Ward understood that the eradication of those racist notions would help to relieve the suffering in the world.

In light of the foregoing it is my intention to demonstrate how Ward's doctrine of Christology provided the guiding force for his participation in the struggle for social and moral reform. Through this discussion I hope to illumine the specific dimension of Christology as it applied to one black abolitionist--Samuel R. Ward.

For purposes of clarity the book begins with a discussion of the biographical features that help to create Ward's doctrine of Christology and then the study turns to an analysis of his rhetoric.

It is important to note that this study has been recognized and cited in *The Black Press* by Roland Wolseley. In addition a microfilm, an index, and three volumes of *The Black Abolitionist Papers* edited by C. Peter Ripley identify most of Ward's public discourses and his reformist actions.

I have included "Notes" at the end of each chapter. After the concluding chapter there are two examples of speeches Ward delivered in public, a bibliography, and an index.

NOTES

1. Charles H. Wesley, "The Negroes of New York in the Emancipation Movement," *The Journal of Negro History* 23 (1939): 80.

2. Otey Scruggs, "Alexander Crummell (1819-1898), Pioneer, Black Intellectual, Cultural Materialist, and Founder of St. Luke's Church," Paper read before the Black Episcopalians of Washington, D.C., March, 1974.

3. Carol George, "Richard Allen and the Rise of the Independent Black Church Movement, 1738-1837," (Ph.D. Diss., Syracuse Univ. 1970).

4. Earl Ofari, *Let Your Motto Be Resistance* (Boston: Beacon Press, 1972), p. 51.

5. For an excellent survey of Christology see: Sydney Cave, *The Doctrine of the Work of Christ* (Nashville, Tennessee: Cokesbury Press, 1937).

6. Cave, p. 43.

7. James H. Cone, *Black Theology and Black Power* (New York: The Seabury Press, 1969), p. 35.

8. Samuel Ringgold Ward, *Autobiography of a Fugitive Negro* (Reprint) (Chicago: Johnson Publishing, Co., 1970), p. 33.

9. Ward, (1970), p. 73.

10. Timothy L. Smith, *Revivalism and Social Reform* (New York: Harper & Row, 1957), p. 152.

11. *The Impartial Citizen*, January 23, 1850. This antislavery tract is in the holdings of The American Antiquarian Society in Worcester, Massachusetts.

Samuel R. Ward in his early years.

Chapter 1
The Early Years

Many factors in the childhood and young adulthood of the Reverend Mister Samuel Ringgold Ward bear on his subsequent career as a religious reformer. The offspring of devoutly religious parents Ward associated regularly with several leading activists of the African American church, he attended a religiously-oriented school for African American youth, and he participated in church-connected reform activities. When these factors are examined closely the formulation of Ward's doctrine of Christology becomes clearer.

Born on the Eastern Shore of Maryland on October 17, 1817 of slave parents Samuel was the second of three boys.[1] The eldest died prior to Samuel's birth and the youngest died in 1838 in New York city. In 1820 Ward and his parents escaped slavery and journeyed to New Jersey.

Devout Christians, Ward's parents reared him in The Faith. He remembered his early childhood spent in Greenwich, Cumberland County, New Jersey from 1820 to 1826--a time in which he worked happily alongside his father, William Ward, in the family garden. Ward recalled that his father taught him "Some valuable lessons--the use of the hoe, to spell in three syllables, and to read the first chapter of John's gospel, and figures."[2]

The message contained in the gospel of John left an indelible imprint on Samuel. Unlike the other gospels John is more concerned with bringing out the significance of Jesus's works. The following excerpt is illustrative: "For God sent his Son into the world, not to condemn the world, but so that through Him the world might be saved."[3] Throughout John's sacred writings the mystery of the Incarnation and the miracle of the Resurrection appear to dominate John's thought.[4] Alexander Jones, editor of *The Jerusalem Bible*, agrees that John's gospel is the most representative of the true meaning of the life of Christ. The elder Ward could not have chosen a more appropriate gospel to teach his future son -- a future Christian Activist.

Samuel once described his father as having woolly hair, small, handsome features and a height of approximately five feet ten inches. He had a well formed physique, a cheerful disposition, and a quiet unassuming nature. Samuel resembled his father physically, but his personality rarely exhibited a quiet and unassuming manner. Samuel had, in fact, an excitable nature which reinforced his desire to abolish slavery--a character trait he may have inherited from his mother. She shared with her husband membership in the Methodist church--"though a lover of all Christian denominations."[5] Ward's mother Ann had an assertive and proactive nature which Samuel recalled his mother telling him that when the family lived in slavery she spent a great deal of time praying by herself.

The Holy Bible occupied an important part of their family life. The reading lessons Ward took from his father were put to use immediately; he read the Scriptures to his mother upon her request. "I first read the Bible to my beloved mother, I read in her countenance (what I then could not read in the book) what the Bible was to her."[6] By coincidence young Samuel became ill at about the time the master threatened to sell him.[7] But the master withdrew his threat due to the illness and ordered Ann Ward to stay with her child.

Fearing separation from her family Ann planned and executed their escape from slavery. Reflecting on the journey Samuel related that their religious faith aided them in their escape. He said they were"drawn and stimulated by the hope of freedom, while all the while trusting in and committing themselves to Him who is God of the oppressed."[8] Then, the Wards took up residence in New Jersey.

Inasmuch as the threat of kidnapping and slave-catching became increasingly dangerous in New Jersey the Ward family moved to New York City in 1826. Ward and his family arrived in New York City at a time of transition among the abolitionists. The reformers then present in the city were being supplanted by a more militant group of African Americans. The older group were by no means high-pressure reformers; their approach to reform represented a moderate and conciliatory position. The new spirit spreading through New York sought liberation at a more aggressive pace. It did not reflect the style of the old guard who believed that "slavery was a sin for which God would eventually exact retribution."[9] They maintained a gradualist philosophy trusting to what they anticipated to be the inevitable arrival of egalitarian principles. In brief, these blacks expected slavery to disappear by slow degrees at some future, unspecified time. In short, they looked for events to take care of themselves.

Unlike their predecessors the newer breed of activists pursued more vigorous reform tactics. This group held conventions on an annual basis to establish communications in the black community; they published newspapers to transmit social, political, and religious news to black people; and, they took advantage of the educational opportunities provided by the New York African Free-School.[10] The pressures for change had been mounting for years and a group consciousness among African Americans began to establish itself.

The historian Charles Wesley--mentioned earlier--reported that, "The leaders of the first period, those of the thirties, gave way to those of another period, those of the forties and fifties. Wright, Bell, Paul, Williams, and Ruggles were succeeded by Garnet, Ward, Douglass, Ray, and Smith."[11]

In due time Ward became acquainted with these reformers. Theodore Wright, Pastor of the First Presbyterian Church in New York, joined with Ward and others to organize a convention in Albany, New York to be conducted exclusively by blacks.[12] Furthermore Wright and Ward were recognized for their leadership when they were elected to be two of the American Missionary Association's five vice-presidents.[13]

During Ward's young adulthood in New York City he maintained contact with African American activists. That Wesley included him in the second group of reformers attests to his having a well-earned reputation among his black peers. He participated in activities with his cousin Henry Highland Garnet when on several occasions they spoke at antislavery meetings. Ward and Garnet claimed membership in the Liberty Party--a political party comprised of abolitionist voters who were working for the repeal of the fugitive slave laws and the fugitive slave trade.[14] Along with Ward, Garnet worked as an agent for the American Missionary Association.[15]

Ward communicated frequently with Frederick Douglass, the standard-bearer of black emancipation and editor-owner of the leading antislavery tract *The North Star*. Both men appeared frequently on the platforms of the antislavery speaking circuit--often they shared the same platform. They are best remembered for their debate on the constitutionality of slavery at the Broadway Tabernacle in New York City in May 1849.[16] Deeply impressed with Ward's oratorical skills Douglass remarked: "As an orator and thinker he was vastly superior, I thought, to any of us, and being perfectly black and of unmixed African descent, the splendors of his intellect went directly to the glory of race."[17] Additionally, Douglass and Ward wrote letters to each other's newspapers on several occasions maintaining a dialogue on reform.

Another activist, Charles B. Ray participated in activities similar to Ward's. A member of the clergy and an agent of the American Antislavery Society Ray helped Ward and Wright organize the African American convention in Albany, New York in the summer of 1840.

Other black abolitionist contemporaries in New York City were: Alexander Crummell, James McCune Smith, and James W.C. Pennington. That they were all church-connected, lay or clerical, as well as active participants in the emancipation movement appeared to be the ties that held them together.

Crummell whom Ward referred to as "One of my dear schoolfellows,"[18] was a free-born black considered to be one of the most intellectual of black reformers. Orator, writer, traveler, and later in life, the rector of Saint Luke's church in Washington, D.C. Crummell took his Baccalaureate degree from Queen's College, Cambridge, England in 1852.[19]

A civil libertarian, black physician, and graduate of the University of Scotland, James McCune Smith's writings and speeches were published in several antislavery newspapers. At a meeting in New York City in May of 1850 Ward said he "lectured to black men on the same evening in Shiloh Church. Mr. C.L. Remond and Dr. J. McCune Smith following me in their usual power and eloquence."[20]

An author and ordained minister The Reverend James W.C. Pennington received the Doctor of Divinity degree from the University of Heidelberg. Years before he had escaped from slavery and met a Quaker who helped to educate him. Subsequently Pennington moved to New York and taught African American children in New Town, Long Island eventually being replaced at the school by Ward. Pennington later became the first pastor of the Shiloh Presbyterian Church in New York City from 1847 to 1855. During that time he authored *The Fugitive Blacksmith*, one of the foremost slave narratives of the time.[21] Moreover Ward, Pennington, and other activists were in attendance at the inaugural meeting of the American Missionary Association. On several occasions these men presented discourses from the same public platform.[22]

Ward, then, resided in New York City in a time of reform actions, that is, when a new generation of black activists emerged on the scene to accelerate the attack on slavery. As Ward became involved in the movement toward the abolition of slavery he embraced a philosophy of African American Christian activism wherein he perfected his theory of social and moral reform.

Prior to participating in reform activities Ward and many of his fellow abolitionists received their education at the New York African Free-School. The religious portion of the school's curricula provided much motivation for Ward to develop his theory of Christology. He remarked: "I was placed at a public school in Mulberry Street, taught by Mr. C.C. Andrew and subsequently by Mister Adams, a Quaker gentleman, from both of whom I received great kindness. Doctor A. Libolt, my last preceptor in that school, placed me under lasting obligation."[23]

Instituted by the New York Manumission Society in 1787 the school sought to become a benevolent association dedicated to the improvement of black people, viewing with "commiseration the poor African slave."[24] Moreover, the academy dedicated itself to exerting all lawful means to ameliorate all slaves sufferings and, inevitably "free him (sic) from bondage."[25]

Instruction at the school followed the Lancasterian system which intended to train large numbers of students. Doubtless the system accommodated the school because it had large numbers of students and a small faculty. The philosophy of the African Free-School aimed to produce students with a strong social conscience. To help the student achieve the desired social and moral concern the school involved the family in its activities by distributing pamphlets containing guidelines for child care and social deportment. The school encouraged the parents to read the Scriptures frequently in their home and to attend church regularly.[26]

The instructions received at the school show a strong resemblance to an editorial Ward wrote for his antislavery tract, *The Impartial Citizen:*

> On the other hand, if in the midst of our present depressions and discouragements, we shall cultivate self-respect, dignity of demeanor, refinement of manners, intelligence, morality and

> religion; if we shall be industrious. frugal, temperate, chaste, we shall be an elevated people, in spite of all the pro-slavery negro-hate this boasted, lying Republic is disgraced and degraded with.[27]

The religious emphasis espoused by the African Free-School reinforced the moral training that prevailed in the Ward household. The school and the home were lasting influences on young Samuel.

Moreover, the teachers taught Christianity in the broad sense as no one particular denomination dominated their courses of study. The fifty-third chapter of Isaiah appeared to be a popular Scriptural reading at the school. Its central message is: "On Him lies a punishment that brings us peace, through His wounds we are healed."[28] The religious training emphasized the meaning of Christ's work.

The meaning of Christ's work appeared often in the discourses of the members of the "Class of Merit." A class that appparently came to be an important part of the school. Students with high scholastic aptitudes were placed in this "Class of Merit." As special students they were expected to set good examples for the less gifted. The requisites for membership in the class consisted of: good character, an indication of ample progress in studies, and approval of the instructor. The members of the class supervised pupil deportment, maintained personal cleanliness among the students, and kept watch over the health of the students.

A group pride pervaded the members of the class. That pride evidenced itself when one member spoke to his classmates and declared that they should thank God for their good fortune in being part of the class. He reminded them of the need to retain a high moral character through life. He complimented them on their high mutual regard which evidently went beyond simple friendship.[29] Above all, the students in the class were expected to be potential leaders. They were taught that they were to help the needy, maintain a high regard for each other, and give frequent expression of dislike for "all that is mean and vulgar."[30] Ward and his classmates from the African Free-School went on to employ that training later on in life for the betterment of all men and women.

Other classmates at the Free-School who became luminaries in the movement were Thomas Sidney and Charles Reason. Sidney expressed his concern for liberty when he recited a poem entitled "On Freedom" at the school on October 21, 1828.[31] Seven years later on

Independence Day in Plymouth, New Hampshire Sidney spoke at a public meeting, and, on the same program were fellow Free-School graduates Crummell and Garnet.[32]

In addition, Charles Reason graduated from the New York African Free-School and soon took a position after his graduation as a professor of *belles lettres* at New York Central College founded in 1849 in McGrawville, New York by the American Baptist Free Mission Society. A coeducational institution New York Central College welcomed students of any race, color, or religion. The faculty and students of Central College were pledged to antislavery.[33] Many of the graduates of the New York Free-School participated in humanitarian activities subsequent to their leaving the academy. It is clear that the New York African Free-School made a long term influence on Ward and the group of black scholars with whom he associated. The moral instruction, the religious teachings, and the demands for personal discipline and high moral character established the groundwork for his later occupation as a Christian Abolitionist.

In 1833 Ward worked as a clerk for Thomas L. Jennings, an active reformer. One of the first officers of the Phoenix Society--an African American benevolent organization--Jennings chaired their convention in New York City in 1833. Also, Jennings worked to remove the suffrage restriction on blacks. Jennings also sued the Third Avenue Railway Company for ejecting his daughter from one of its cars. He won the case and that victory led to the abolition of caste on cars in four out of five of the railroads operating in the city.[34]

David Ruggles, another well-known figure in antislavery circles employed Ward for a short time. He first established his business in New York City in 1829 where he owned and operated a grocery store until 1833. After witnessing the deplorable conditions among the African Americans Ruggles closed his business and joined the New York Committee of Vigilance, became an agent for an antislavey newspaper, and worked arduously for the New York Anti-Slavery Society. One of Ruggles's more notable acts involved aiding the fugitive slave Frederick Douglass in his bid for freedom. At Ruggles's home the Reverend J.W.C. Pennington married Douglass to Anna Murray.[35]

White as well as black abolitionists influenced Ward. In 1834 he visited New Haven, Connecticut to listen to Simeon S. Jocelyn, a white minister lecture on slavery. Ward reported on Jocelyn's discourse: "When a lecture was announced to be delivered on the subject of slavery by that gentleman, I was but too glad to hear him. I learned to love him as a child; I now have the honour of his friendship as a man. His was the first antislavery lecture I ever heard."[36] Jocelyn occupied his time by being a conductor on the underground railroad in Connecticut, and founding both the New Haven Anti-Slavery Society and the New Haven Temple Street Church. A selfless man he spurned a lucrative position as an engraver to study theology, enter the ministry, and participate in social and moral reform.[37] Jocelyn's church operated as an abolitionist center, a place for meetings, a station on the underground railroad, and a location for monthly prayer meetings. Frequently Ward reminded his audiences that he had close friendships and had been acquainted with the above-mentioned activists.

Ward's personal ethic of a love for all men and women approached annihilation when he witnessed a riot during an antislavery meeting held at Chatham Street Chapel in New York City on July 4, 1834. Abolitionists met to hear a scheduled speech by David Paul Brown, a "Well known champion of freedom" whose topic would be the principles enunciated in the Declaration of Independence. A Philadelphia activist-lawyer Brown had been honored for his efforts in aiding runaway slaves.[38] Before Brown could speak a mob of colonizationists broke up the meeting. It happened this way: Soon after the American Antislavery Society gathered at the Chatham Chapel the choir opened the meeting with a song, then there followed a reading of the declaration of sentiments by Lewis Tappan, a successful businessman-abolitionist and friend of the African American. As Tappan reached the concluding paragraph a gang of toughs who had gathered at the chapel door began to mimic him. Brown then rose to speak but he was shouted down. Brown persisted but to no avail.[39] The choir attempted unsuccessfully to bring the meeting to order with a song. An enraged Tappan sent for the Mayor. When the Mayor arrived with the police he saw no reason to intevene in the melee since the intruders were only a "few low fellows" creating a mild disturbance.[40]

The New York City newspapers repeatedly misrepresented the incident at the Chatham Street Chapel. Unsympathetic Editors of two New York City papers, *The Commercial Advertiser* and *The Courier and Enquirer* registered complaints that the meetings had been instigated by amalgamators with incendiary placards. Amalgamators being individual troublemakers who did not support an integrated society.[41] The abolitionists knew however that adherents of the American Colonization Society were responsible for intruding on the meeting.[42] A poster found near the chapel on the morning of the incident read in part: "Remember freemen what this society aim (sic) at--The Disunion of the States. Signed Many Friends of the Country."[43]

The Liberator, an antislavery newspaper edited by the Boston abolitionist-firebrand William Lloyd Garrison alleged that William L. Stone editor of the American Colonization Society's propaganda organ *The Commercial Advertiser* printed enough biased information to cause a riot at the chapel. Statements printed in the paper were: "The society is designed to foment a civil war in the South." "The scheming fanatics or knaves who professing to advocate immediate abolition of slavery have busied themselves for months past in disseminating their absurd doctrines." More comments were: "There are mobs of abolitionists now nightly engaged in deeds of violence." "Will the citizens of this city longer submit to have their brethren attacked by the abetted mobs of negroes; their ears harshly assailed with the vile and debased proposition of a general amalgamation of color?"[44] Ward observed that the rioters had perpetrated their act "Just fifty-eight years from the very hour that the Declaration of 1776 was made."[45]

Three days following that incident there occurred another riot caused by the same mob. On July 7, 1834 black abolitionists held a meeting in the same chapel to celebrate the emancipation of slaves in New York State. The riot started because of a mix-up in the scheduling events at the Chatham Chapel. A group of black men arranged to hire the chapel at the same time as some white men. The people who arranged the meetings thought the chapel sexton had informed everyone of the change but the vice-president of the white people's group claimed he had not been apprised of the change. When he entered the hall with several others and saw the meeting in progress he ordered his men to clear the hall. And, when the blacks refused to leave violence erupted.[46] What followed turned into a violent event. Benches were thrown from the balcony, chairs were broken over heads, and people on both sides were injured. Blacks succeeded in driving the whites from the hall but within a few minutes the mob returned with reinforcements overpowering the blacks. Those blacks who remained--Ward among them--were jailed and charged with fomenting the riot. Ward's avowal in response to his incarceration is significant: "That imprisonment," he asserted, "initiated me into the antislavery fraternity."[47]

Ward's youth in New York City and the surrounding areas laid the foundation for his subsequent social and moral reform activities. He grew up in an environment that included individuals who manifested a deep social conscience. His parents reared him to be a responsible Christian; his education reflected strong Christian principles; many of his associates were black church leaders; and, as a young man he would study and become a licensed preacher.

By 1839, Ward enlisted as an agent for the American Anti-Slavery Society. The next phase of Ward's life involved his travels on the speaking circuit addressing the problems of human rights, especially the institution of slavery.

NOTES

1. Several eminent black reformers were born in Maryland. They were: J.W.C. Pennington, Henry Highland Garnet, Benjamin Banneker, Harriet Tubman, and Frederick Douglass. See Lerone Bennett, Jr., *Before the Mayflower* (Baltimore, Maryland: Penguin Books, 1966), pp. 146-47.

2. Ward, (1970), p. 20.

3 Alexander Jones, ed., *The Jerusalem Bible* (New York: Doubleday & Co., Inc., 1966), p. 151 (N.T.).

4. Jones (1966), p. 141.

5. Ward, (1970), p. 6.

6. Ward, (1970), p. 20.

7. The slaves knew that plantation owners in the deep South were especially cruel in their treatment of slaves. Consequently, the slave feared deeply being sold "down the river."

8. Ward, (1970), p. 18,

9. Benjamin Quarles, *Black Abolitionists* (New York: Oxford University Press, 1969), p. 68.

10. Wesley, (1939), pp. 65-103.

11. Wesley, (1939), pp. 65-103.

12. Ofari, (1972), p. 15.

13. Quarles, (1969), p. 79.

14. Quarles, (1969), p. 183.

15. See *The Impartial Citizen* for 1849 and 1850, especially October 5, 1850.

16. Benjamin Quarles, *Frederick Douglass* (New York: Atheneum, 1968), p. 104. See also John W. Blassingame, ed., *The Frederick Douglass Papers* vols. I through IV (New Haven: Yale University Press, 1979, 1982, 1985, 1987). A brief account of the debate between Douglass and Ward is in volume II of *The Frederick Douglass Papers* see pages 193-197.

17. Frederick Douglass, *Life and Times of Frederick Douglass* (London: Collier-Macmillan, Ltd., 1962), p. 277.

18. Ward, (1970), p. 44.

19. Scruggs, (1974).

20. *The Impartial Citizen*, May 29, 1850.

21. Dumas Malone, ed., *Dictionary of American Biography* (New York: Charles Scribner's Sons, 1934), p. 441.

22. Quarles, (1969), p. 79.

23. Ward, (1970), p. 21. All of these men were instructors at the New York African Free-School.

24. Charles C. Andrews, *The History of the New York African Free-School* (New York: Negro University Press, 1969), p. 7.

25. Andrews, (1969), p. 8.

26. Andrews, (1969), p. 10.

27. *The Impartial Citizen*, March 14, 1849.

28. Jones, (1966), p. 1228, (O.T.).

29. Andrews, (1969), p. 143-44.

30. Andrews, (1969), p. 84.

31. Andrews, (1969), p. 65.

32. Quarles, (1969), pp. 90-91.

33. *The Impartial Citizen*, August 1, 1849; *The North Star*, April, 26, 1850.

34. *The Anglo-African Magazine*, v. 1, 1859, p. 127.

35. For an account of Ruggles's antislavery activities see: Dorothy B. Porter, "David Ruggles, An Apostle of Human Rights," *Journal of Negro History* 27 (1943).

36. Ward, (1970), p. 35.

37. Horatio T. Strother, *The Underground Railroad in Connecticut* (Middletown, Connecticut: Wesleyan University Press, 1962).

38. Quarles, (1969), p. 166.

39. *The Liberator*, July 12, 1834.

40. For a full discussion of anti-abolition mobs see: Leonard L. Richards, *Gentlemen of Property and Standing: Anti-Abolition Mobs in Jacksonian America* (New York: Oxford University Press, 1970.)

41. Richards, (1970), p. 117.

42. For a discussion of the American Colonization Society see: Philip C. Wander, "Salvation Through Separation: The Image of the Negro in the American Colonization Society," *The Quarterly Journal of Speech* 57 (1971): 57-87.

43. *The Liberator*, July 12, 1834.

44. *The Liberator*, July 26, 1834. In Richards (1970) he states that the problem of immediatism or instant freedom for the slaves has been advanced as the reason for anti-abolition mobs. But beneath all of the turmoil rests the actual reasons--that of amalgamation or miscegenation. His book is well documented to prove this point.

45. Ward, (1970), p. 36.
46. *The Liberator*, July 12, 1834.
47. Ward, (1970), p. 37.

Chapter 2

The First Pastorate

In 1836 Ward moved to Newark, New Jersey to teach school. After two and half years he met and married a Miss Reynolds of New York. In October of 1838 Ward's wife gave birth to Samuel Ringgold Ward, Junior. "My wife," or "Mrs. Ward" (He never mentioned her first name) apparently did not converse very much as he reported that she had a "stillness which borders on taciturnity."[1] That character trait evidently pleased Ward as he claimed a close relationship with her.

Shortly after his marriage the Wards moved to Poughkeepsie, New York and there he taught for a short time at the city's Colored Lancasterian School. He left teaching in 1839 and became a licensed preacher with the New York Congregational Association.[2] Early in the preaching career he encountered racial prejudice and decided to look for another occupation. "My determination was formed to leave the country. I accordingly wrote to a Mr. Burnley of the Trinidad Legislature, a relation of the late Joseph Hume, Esq., M.P. who kindly encouraged my going to that island."[3] Next, Ward requested a letter of recommendation from a former acquaintance and Congregational Minister-Abolitionist the Reverend Mister Joshua Leavitt. Leavitt responded by asking Ward if he would be interested in working for the antislavery cause. Ward accepted the offer and took an appointment as an antislavery agent for the American Anti-Slavery Society. This occupation connected appropriately to his previous participation in social and moral reform.

Ward began working for the Society in 1839, the same year it severed into two splinter groups--the New York Anti-Slavery Society and the American Anti-Slavery Society. The latter group included William Lloyd Garrison and his associates. The former group included Gerrit Smith, James G. Birney, William Goodell and Beriah Green.[4] Garrison's members criticized the church vehemently, moreover, some of their criticism did not fall within the purview of abolitionism. Additionally they did not advocate the power of the vote to fight slavery. That view directly contradicted the New Yorkers who believed that to gain reform there had to be political and religious involvement. Inasmuch as Ward favored the religious and political approach he joined the New York Anti-Slavery Society. He supported their belief in Christ-like labor, God's interposition in slavery, and the inevitable deliverance from evil. His thoughts about the matter were: "I had the unspeakable pleasure of making the acquaintance of some of its most distinguished members and officers, and, at the same time, of avoiding official connection with the quarrels which divided the Anti-Slavery Society in 1840, and the subsequent dissension among them."[5]

In February of 1841 Ward traveled to Western New York on a speaking tour and spoke at a Congregational Church in South Butler, Wayne County. Notably impressed with Ward's speaking the people in South Butler offered Ward the pastorate of the church. He negotiated with them and accepted the position in April of that year. In the Fall, the Congregational church ordained and inducted Samuel R. Ward into the South Butler church ministry.[6]

The church building in which Ward administered his duties no longer stands. As late as 1895 however, the building served as a dwelling.[7] The village is situated three miles north of the direct railroad route between Syracuse and Rochester, New York. Ward observed that the politically active and thriving community of South Butler boasted of a saw mill, a grist mill, a furnace factory, a plow factory, a tannery, several mechanics, two dry goods stores, a Temperance Hotel, four male and two female physicians, one justice of the peace, a large school and three churches.[8] Today, South Butler is a sparsely inhabited village twelve miles north of the New York State Thruway.

Ward displayed enthusiasm and dedication in his new undertaking. Since the appointment to an all-white congregation attracted much attention, "both pro and con" he thought it vastly important that he conduct himself in a responsible manner. He wished to perform a credible job so that white detractors would not gain satisfaction from mistakes he might make. In his good behavior he would be able to speak out against slavery since no other matters interfered. He intended to demonstrate that African American's had the ability to do God's will as capably as other groups.

While Ward preached regularly to his own congregation in South Butler he preached frequently elsewhere. He would visit African Americans in the surrounding area and deliver sermons on character development. His method of preaching on character improvement entertained the notion that blacks must forgive whites as Christ forgave those who sinned against Him. Ward held the conviction that the African American's intense religious feeling could induce white people to express love more than hate. He subscribed to the idea that an expression of love can be disarming to the unrighteous and thus stimulate creative thought. And, more importantly he approved of the notion that forgiveness plays a crucial role in the black person's character development. Ward explained that if black-white relations were more amicable then each side would learn from the other.

Ward referred to himself as a "Christian Abolitionist" that is a religiously-oriented reformer as opposed to the Garrison group who believed the church only sanctioned the continuation of slavery. Hence, the unabashed slaveowners who were members of churches created a constant annoyance in Ward's mind. His Christian responsibility consisted of working within the confines of the church to persuade slaveowners to free their bondmen and bondwomen. He did not advise the slaveowners to leave the church; he hoped to dissuade them from keeping their slaves. "Remain in the church," he would tell the ruling class, "but liberate your slaves." He despised their method of contributing funds to the church, serving as respected men and women in the community, and owning slaves. The incoming money restrained some clergy from speaking out against the slavocrats. Needless to say the practice frustrated Ward who spent much of his time speaking out against the hypocritical clergy and the evil slaveowners. To make matters worse slaveholders contributed to charities, sent money to missionaries overseas, and gave money to the poor in Europe while they participated in the practice of slaveholding at home.[9]

An additional bone of contention to Ward concerned the hypocrisy of the Northern clergy. If they condemned slavery from the pulpit it would be in the abstract. But if they criticized antislavery efforts it would be in the concrete. When the northern preachers were pressed to take a stand they would proclaim that some "sins are not to be preached against"--referring of course, to slavery.

In his preaching Ward took on the benevolent societies. He exposed the American Tract Society for carefully avoiding the publishing of anything critical of slavery. Moreover, he exposed the American Bible Society for not distributing the Scriptures among the slave population when they had pledged that "every" family in the United States would receive a volume. And, he said the powerful American Sunday School Union had pro-slavery persons as its leaders. Lastly, he noted that the American Board of Commissioners for Foreign Missions supported slavery. His oratory blasted away at several religious organizations who were subject to control by slaveowning authorities within their ranks.

What reasons were given for the existence of such conditions? Ward explained that men and women did not wish to create any friction in their church community. Nor did they wish to forfeit stable economic and social conditions even if it meant enslavement. When disharmony over slavery surfaced Ward observed that the abolitionists usually received the blame. Pro-slavery forces claimed that abolitionists intended to disintegrate the Union. But in reality the fear of splitting the North and South came in second to the actual fear of race mixing.

Ward recognized another societal evil--that of caste. He saw it as a result of the white person's contempt of the black person. "Surely," he said, "if they believe him (sic) to be an *equal brother man*, such miserable pretexts for, and defiance of, the doing of the mightiest wrongs against him, would never for a moment be thought of."[10] Ward understood caste as the exclusion of African Americans from positions of power. Caste enraged Ward especially when he observed the careful arrangements people concocted in order to keep blacks from attaining access to a higher status in society. For instance, in 1849 he witnessed the white power structure in Rochester, New York as it worked to strengthen the caste system. He wrote a sarcastic editorial exposing the Rochester School Board for its part in perpetuating caste:

> In Rochester, the School Board would doubtless have concluded to allow black and white children to attend the common schools together, had not the trustees of one of the colored churches, for the paltry sum of one hundred dollars, fitted up a low damp basement for the debasement of the colored children, that providing means for a separate, a caste-

> erected school, to accommodate the very negro-hate which treads them down.[11]

Alexander Crummell, one-time classmate of Ward's had some words of observation about what the "caste spirit" declared: "You Negroes may get learning; you may get property; you may have churches and religion; but this is your limit! This is a white man's government! No matter how many millions you may number, we Anglo-Saxons are to rule![12] Caste had to be dealt with realistically for both Crummell and Ward.

A typical sermon Ward presented to his South Butler congregation would be as follows: He repeatedly told his audience that slavery had to be abolished. He asked his listeners very basic questions to get them to think about the problem. He would ask: "Is it not the buying and selling of the image of God? Is it not brutal and demeaning? Did not Christ denounce this evil? He preached that Jesus did not want one person to own another--"It violates the ten commandments," he said. He would cry out the words of Jesus knowing that the congregation could recall the words from the Bible: "Inasmuch as ye did it (or did not) to the least of my brethren, ye did it (or did it not), unto me." If Ward had one mission in South Butler it was his deep concern for the fate of the slave. He thought since he had a more than average knowledge of slavery it became his responsibility to educate his auditors about the peculiar institution of human bondage.

Also, Ward purposely supported the political views of the Christian Abolitionists in the sermons to his congregation. He knew that the then existing political parties contradicted their supposedly planned agendas--that is, their claim to freedom and democracy. For example, neither the Whig Party nor the Democratic party took a position on the problem of slavery. But the Christian Abolitionists hoped that those politicians would support the sentiments of the Declaration of Independence. This political situation motivated Ward to become a charter member of the Liberty party, a party that took a definite antislavery position.

As a Christian Abolitionist Ward argued against slavery by telling his churchgoers that if a black man or woman can be enslaved legally, so may other men and women. Ward saw the political system that behaved in this manner as eroding. As a result of the institution of slavery politicians were blocking the right of petition, blocking freedom of the press, blocking free speech, and generally blocking the rights of all men and women.

Ward continued to discuss the slavery problem with his congregation. He said slavery destroyed the liberty of all free men and women. If free people whipped, tarred, feathered, and lynched others, then they in reality were also enslaved by Satan, he said. If as now the African American is arbitrarily placed in bondage then who would be next? He hammered away at that theme during his tenure at South Butler.

The people of South Butler--who had migrated from New England--stood proudly by Ward even in the presence of severe criticism from outside detractors who scoffed at the idea of an African American preaching to an Anglo-American congregation. As a consequence of their belief in Ward the congregation made his life there heartwarming and pleasant. Ward's church members in South Butler were enlightened Christians who listened to what he had to say about slavery, then they made up their minds regardless of the pressures of outside influence.

Ward claimed that because of the location of the town of South Butler in the interior of the state the populous ineluctably avoided the opinionated influences of the city. Ward believed this isolation added to their open-mindedness. He recalled numerous happy moments as he spread the word of Jesus in South Butler.

In spite of the fact that Ward's residence in South Butler did not last long, his tenure offered him the opportunity to test several ideas and sharpen further his speaking skills. Subsequent to that two and a half year stint Ward moved to Geneva, New York, when after a brief interlude he received medical treatment to his throat. With that ailment healed he went to Cortlandville, New York to occupy another pastorate. His time in Cortlandville, moreover, represents the years in which his doctrine came to fruition.

NOTES

1. *The Impartial Citizen*, November 21, 1849.

2. Ward, (1970), p. 23.

3. Ward, (1970), p. 38; Ward never explained his relationship with Burnley or Hume.

4. A discussion of the split between the two factions is in: Gerald Sorin, *The New York Abolitionists* (Westport, Connecticut: Greenwood Publishing Corp., 1971).

5. Ward, (1970), p. 41.

6. Ward, (1970), p. 23.

7. George W. Cowles, ed., *Landmarks of Wayne County* Syracuse: D. Mason, 1895), p. 436.

8. *The New York Tribune*, August 27, 1853.

9. Ward, (1970), p. 47.

10. Ward, (1970), p. 50.

11. *The Impartial Citizen*, November 21, 1849.

12. Alexander Crummell, *Africa and America, Addresses and Discourses* (Reprint) (New York: Negro University Press, 1969), p. 55.

Chapter 3

The Prominent African American Leader

Ward's years spent in Cortlandville, New York appear to be the most prolific in his career. All of his previous training and experience culminated in reformist activities at that point in his life. For example, in addition to pastoring Cortlandville's Congregational Church he edited two antislavery newspapers: *The True American* from 1847 to 1848 and *The Impartial Citizen* from 1849 to 1851. The latter functioned as a propaganda organ for the Liberty Party in which Ward worked as a traveling agent and spokesperson. In the meantime he held also the position of vice-president for the American Missionary Association. As a consequence of this notably busy life one of his renowned contemporaries Martin R. Delany ranked Ward as one of the outstanding leaders of the period.[1]

Similar to many abolitionist editors Ward's first venture into the area of journalism proved disastrous. The publication of *The True American* lasted but one year. To solve his financial difficulties Ward joined forces and merged with Stephen Myers editor of *The Northern Star and Colored Farmer* of Albany, New York.[2] Both men discontinued publication of their respective papers and used their talents to produce *The Impartial Citizen* in Syracuse, New York. To keep the newspaper solvent Ward intended to increase the readership of the *Citizen* to two thousand.[3] Myers in the meantime kept busy in many circles beyond journalism by participating in politics, by lobbying for voting rights for blacks in New York State, and by operating as an agent for the underground railroad in Albany.[4]

Not unlike other antislavery tracts *The Citizen's* editor usually inserted on the front page a sympathetic politician's speech or a romantic short story in serial form. Advertisements by a Temperance

House, a colored boarding house, a lithography and engraving shop, a bakery, a hardware store, and a lumber company occupied the first column on the front page. These business establishments were either owned by blacks or they were white-owned businesses sympathetic to the antislavery struggle.

On the inside pages of *The Impartial Citizen* could be found letters to the editor, a "Scribblings" column containing short news items, Convention notices, minutes of antislavery meetings, a news from Europe section, religious news, and most importantly, the "Editorial Correspondence" column. These editorials constituted the direct means by which Ward expressed his ideas to his readers. Here he revealed his thoughts to his subscribers by way of chatty, personal, and informative writings. Readers looked forward to Ward's reports of political activities in the cities, towns, and villages that he visited on speaking tours. He gave explicit descriptions of the picturesque countryside and frequently he discussed the need for attention to African American self-elevation and social progress.

As expected Ward attacked slavery through the newspaper but he used his resources in the Liberty Party since that Party's imperative intended to oppose the spread of slavery. One of the main reasons for the members to come together concerned the apparent lack of making slavery a problem by the Whigs and Democrats. Inasmuch as the regular political parties refused to condemn slavery the Liberty Party declared they would criticize the slavocracy. James G. Birney, a Southern born aristocrat and former slaveholder who transformed into a born-again Christian rejected slavery as evil and emerged as the presidential candidate in 1840. He welcomed Thomas Earle as his running mate. In the election of 1840 Birney--who had no political acumen--received 7,069 votes, less than one-tenth of the professed abolitionist leadership. In 1844 the party again chose Birney who received over 62,000 votes. After 1844 the party made some progress reaching its zenith in the election of 1846 when just over 74,000 votes were cast for the Liberty Party nominee in the state contests in New England, Pennsylvania, New York, and a few midwestern states.[5] The party held its final convention in 1847 in Buffalo, New York. Though there were several meetings and conferences held in villages and towns in New York the party's enthusiasm gradually declined and interest faded.[6]

By the next presidential campaign of 1848 the party split into two factions and a new party surfaced--the Free-Soilers. The advocates of free-soil proclaimed as its goals: free soil, free speech, free labor, and free people. Martin Van Buren ran as their candidate for president. Asserting their antislavery stance in principle this new party opposed the expansion of slavery but admitted to its legality where it existed. Now a perplexing problem arose among the African Americans. Should they support the weakened Liberty Party or join the seemingly vigorous Free-Soilers?[7]

Ward vehemently opposed the Free Soil Party on the basis that in his inaugural address Van Buren announced his opposition to the abolition of slavery in the District of Columbia. The majority of black voters however, backed Van Buren since he appeared to be the least harmful of those who stood a chance to win. In a letter to Frederick Douglass's paper, *The North Star* Ward criticized Van Buren for being an "exponent of slavery in the Federal District."[8] Subsequent to a realistic appraisal Ward softened his judgment explaining that Van Buren's platform surpassed the then-existing candidates.[9]

In 1850 the membership of the Liberty Party declined significantly to a dedicated few who persisted in putting together a slate of candidates for the election. Gerrit Smith the upstate New York abolitionist-philanthropist received the nomination for president and Ward the vice-presidential slot.[10] Though unsuccessful in having its candidates win elections the Liberty Party continued to serve as a forum for antislavery agitation.

In his campaign speaking Ward criticized severely the institution of slavery on the grounds that it violated laws set down in the United States Constitution. For example, he referred to the constitutional provision that "No state shall pass any law impairing the right of contracts." As to contracts the one for marriage is the most sacred of all. But it would destroy slavery if it were allowed. The master must have unalterable control over the slave, thus, it is impossible for the owner to support married slaves. Any stricture diminishing control over the slave is not permitted. If the slave has marriage rights then he can control his family and protect his wife. That would counteract the slaveowner's needs. Slavemasters do not want this as a condition as they wish unlimited control over the people under their rule. Ward argued that every single slave state had enacted laws impairing the right of contracts involving slaves.[11]

Ward complained of another violation of Constitutional rights. It forbade the passing of any bill of attainder, that is, any bill which designates that the descendant of the criminal shall be punished. He detested the existence of a universal law in slavery which stated that *the slave shall follow the condition of the mother*. This unwritten law violated rights provided to citizens. He believed no state had the right to violate the Federal Constitution which is the supreme law of the land. To Ward the Constitution did not exist as a pro-slavery document. It represented the highest law in the nation operating as a guideline for every citizen. In addition to speaking out against slavery he occupied much space in the columns of *The Citizen* informing the public of the injustices in bondage of which he knew. His message invariably remained the same: The Constitution will serve the country well; the people need to change their ways.

As mentioned earlier Ward challenged his contemporary abolitionist colleague Frederick Douglass to a debate on the constitutionality of slavery at the Broadway Tabernacle in New York City in 1849[12]. In the contest Ward took the Liberty Party position which supported the Constitution as a valid legal document. Douglass defended the opposite opinion. On the afternoon of May 18th the two black leader-orators debated for several hours, took a break for dinner, and then reconvened for another three and half hours. The debaters alternated by speaking in their turn for thirty minutes. Five speeches were given on both sides.[13]

Douglass had the following remarks about the debate with Ward: "The discussion was something new for us, being the first in which we ever engaged. It, however, proved a very pleasant and agreeable entertainment--one which we will remember with the best of feelings, both to the audience and to our respectable and very talented antagonist."[14] He concluded that Ward exhibited fine debating skills, excellent vocal powers, firm command over his audience, and considerable mental ability. Nevertheless, Douglass commented that Ward failed to convince him of the legality of the Constitution.[15] It is noteworthy however, that Douglass reversed his opinion within two years. In 1851 he stated: "The Constitution was in its letter and spirit an antislavery instrument."[16] In brief, both men came to believe that the Constitution showed itself as being legal; the people were violating its mandates.

Not unlike his antislavery movement colleagues Ward spent much time in his public discourses discussing the Fugitive Slave Bill, especially that segment in the Compromise of 1850. Aimed to blunt the exodus of runaway slaves from the South the bill required all whites to aid in the apprehension of slaves. Not only were those who aided and abetted fugitives fined five hundred dollars and imprisoned for six months but the bill further rewarded law officers who captured the runaways. The bill, said Ward blatantly contradicted provisions in the Constitution inasmuch as the runaway did not receive consideration for a speedy trial. In addition, testimony from a U.S. Marshal or his agent--regardless of the circumstances--would be readily accepted as first-hand evidence against the fugitive. Finally Ward's outrage at the law showed in many of his speeches as he referred to it as a "flagrant abuse" of Constitutional law. His agitation increased as he noted that any magistrate or any specially appointed commissioner had the authority to adjudicate at will.[17]

As Ward traveled the antislavery speaking circuit he purposely mentioned the Fugitive Slave Bill. For example, on one occasion he delighted his audience at Faneuil Hall, Boston as he spoke in defiant terms. His booming voice announced that "if anyone came to take him he had better perform two acts for the benefit of himself and his family. He should first make his will and then make peace with his maker. (loud cheers)"[18] The crowd of listeners received his pronouncement with great applause even though the African Americans in the audience were under great strain. Each and every one of the blacks realized they could be taken off the street at the will of any Federal Marshal.[19] Ward's speech seemed to satisfy them emotionally.

Ward's popularity as a leading reformer allowed him entree to a variety of speaking platforms. Frequently he visited New York Central College in McGrawville. The school admitted students without regard to race, and its faculty represented the Anglo American as well as the African American.[20] Ward would design his talks at the college to proseltyze students to become active Christians. Invited to present a speech at the opening ceremonies of the college in 1849 Ward took the opportunity to relate the ugly prejudice and bigotry that had been perpetrated on his former classmates from the New York African Free School.[21] He said that three of his friends were invited by abolitionists to attend school in Canaan, New Hampshire. When Alexander Crummell, Henry Highland Garnet, and Thomas Sidney attended school prejudice began to appear in the surrounding community. Ward quoted Crummell as stating that: "The whole community for miles around was boiling over with bitterness, ready in cold blood, to shoot down a few black boys."[22]

The unreasonably hostile citizens of Canaan resolved to remove the academy because they said it manifested itself as a public nuisance. In time an angry mob gathered, seized the building, and with ninety yoke of oxen dumped the school into a swamp about a half mile from its site. In his address to the Central College students Ward said in the few years since that terrible event occurred the climate had changed somewhat. But he warned that blacks should be alert to the main cause of antislavery--racism. As a result of the unavailability of finances for African American education and the administration's inability to realize the needed funds the College closed its doors after a few years. Unlike the Canaan, New Hampshire residents the McGrawville inhabitants accepted the college.

Wherever Ward traveled he tried to instill black pride in his audiences as well as dispel the myth of black intellectual inferiority. He spoke of the black people's progress even in the face of the social and economic difficulties: "Where," he wanted to know, "is there another people so discouraged, crippled, and oppressed who have done and are doing so much for self-elevation as we?"[23] He boasted of the first African American professor at New York Central College, Charles L. Reason a graduate of Ward's alma mater the New York African Free-School.

Ward especially enjoyed the fact that accomplished African Americans were not limited to one profession. He described the accomplishments of the people he met on his speaking tours: One evening, for example, he "met a very pleasant company of the elite of the black people of Boston and vicinity."[24] He mentioned a lawyer, Mr. Morris, and a Judge, Mr. Allen both professionals were treated with respect by their colleagues in the legal profession. Unlike some African American in elevated positions Allen and Morris--both light skinned--expressed a sensitivity to the plight of the underprivileged. Ward appreciated that both men had social consciences. As mulattoes--both men--could have selfishly attempted to disaffiliate themselves from the African American community. Ward, himself dark skinned and self-confident admired those who remained loyal to their ethnicity.

Agonizing over the continuous presence of the threat inherent in the Fugitive Slave Bill and the mood of apprehension that it created around the country Ward considered leaving the United States and moving to Canada. An incident that helped aggravate his feelings on this matter occurred as Ward ended a speaking tour in 1851. It happened in Christiana, Pennsylvania. A Reverend Gorsuch went in search of his escaped slave to the house of a black man. The owner of the dwelling refused Gorsuch admittance who in turn fired upon the house with his rifle. Occupants in the house received no injuries but in the return volley Gorsuch received a fatal wound.[25] That incident proved to be one more occasion to encourage Ward's emigration to Canada.

When Ward did journey to Canada his leaving created bitterness among some of his associates. A Syracuse activist charged Ward with leaving the United States owing money to subscribers of his paper *The Impartial Citizen.* The activist Jermain W. Loguen Syracuse underground railroad conductor and teacher wrote a letter to the editor of *The Voice of the Fugitive.* In the letter he asked for an explanation for Ward's sudden departure from the United States. Loguen queried as follows:

> Many of our friends have not forgotten the sudden disappearance of S.R. Ward's Impartial Citizen, which many of them say, has never been explained to them. All paid in advance, some received one paper and some never got any, and so it stands. I tell you friend Bibb, it is a very hard matter for one that is not an editor to get along with such things. Editors can explain it much better than I can. Every man at his trade--it does not seem to be mine to get along with such things.[26]

Astonished when he read the letter Ward then explained to Loguen in a Toronto Hotel his reasons for leaving the United States. He told Loguen the paper ran hopelessly into debt because subscribers would not pay their due bills. Ward said he could not collect as much "as a tenth" of the outstanding amount due him. As a consequence authorities in Boston apprehended Ward for debts he could not pay. That is why he declared bankruptcy.[27] "Such was my condition," asserted Ward, "when the 'Jerry' case drove me from my native country." The story Ward told about the Citizen explained the situation of many African American antislavery tracts. Sooner or later many papers went out of business because editors and publishers encountered financial problems.

The "Jerry" case to which Ward referred concerned the apprehension of William Henry, a cooper and fugitive slave residing in Syracuse. Apprehended under the Fugitive Slave Law, Henry--known as Jerry--escaped to Kingston, Ontario, Canada subsequent to being aided by sympathetic abolitionists from Syracuse. The Federal government served notice that anyone involved in the escape would be arrested. Inasmuch as Ward participated in that rendering he decided to elude the Federal Marshals and follow Jerry into Canada.[28]

Following Jerry into Canada concluded Ward's ministry in the United States. His tenure in Cortlandville reflected his full maturity as a Christian Abolitionist. While there he became an eminent black leader by participating in every phase of social and moral reform. He traveled extensively preaching and lecturing in almost every town and village in western and central New York. He published two antislavery newspapers and participated vigorously in the abolitionist activities of the Liberty Party. His Christology however remained at the core of his life. He believed he pleased God by his engagement in Christ's work in Cortlandville. As he wrote at the time: "To do good to man (sic) is to serve God. Christ says: 'Ye cannot serve God and Mammon.'"[29]

NOTES

1. See the letter Martin R. Delany wrote to *The North Star* for June 27, 1850.

2. Sylvia G. Faibisoff and Abigail S. Kelly, "Bibliography of Newspapers in Fourteen New York State Counties," *New York History* (1973): 94.

3. Ronald K. Burke, "THE IMPARTIAL CITIZEN of Samuel Ringgold Ward," *Journalism Quarterly* (1972): 759-760.

4. Quarles, (1969), Chapter IV.

5. Theodore C. Smith, *The Liberty and Free-Soil Parties in the Northwest* (New York: Russell & Russell, 1967).

6. See *The Impartial Citizen* for 1849 and 1850 for notices of local party meetings.

7. Quarles, (1969), p. 185.

8. *The North Star*, September 1, 1848.

9. *The North Star*, September 15, 1848.

10. *The Impartial Citizen*, November 9, 1850.

11. *The Impartial Citizen*, July 25, 1849.

12. *The Impartial Citizen*, July 4, 1849.

13. Quarles, (1968), p. 104.

14. *The North Star*, May 25, 1849.

15. Douglass, (1962), pp. 259-260.

16. Douglass, (1962), pp. 259-260.

17. See the many issues of *The Impartial Citizen* which contain discussions by Ward about the Fugitive Slave Law.

18. Carter G. Woodson, *Negro Orators and Their Orations.* Reprint. (New York: Russell & Russell, 1969), p. 195.

19. Quarles, (1969), p. 79.

20. Quarles, (1969), p. 114.

21. Gerrit Smith Miller Papers, Syracuse University Library, hereafter referred to as GSMP. *First and Second Annual Report of the New York Central College*, July 1849, 1850.

22. Alexander Crummell, *Africa and America--Addresses and Discourses.* Reprint. (New York: Negro University Press, 1969), p. 299.

23. *The Impartial Citizen*, December 3, 1849.

24. *The Impartial Citizen*, April 17, 1850.

25. Ward, (1970), p. 83.

26. *The Voice of the Fugitive*, July 29, 1852. A microfilmed file of this paper for January 1, 1851 to December 16, 1852 is in the Burton Historical Collection of the Detroit Public Library. Issues for January 1, 15, 21, March 21 25, and November 5, 1851 are in the library of the University of Western Ontario.

27. Ward's residence in Massachusetts is explained in the following excerpt from a letter he wrote to Gerrit Smith. "I am impressed with the duty of lecturing in New England for a year or two, to come. Some desire me to publish *the Citizen* in Boston. Certain it is that there is nothing reliable in New England. I shall consult my friends on the subject and act as seems best." GSMP Syracuse University, Ward to Smith, April 30, 1850.

28. For a more detailed account of the Jerry Rescue, see Earl E. Sperry, *The Jerry Rescue*, Syracuse, New York: Onondaga Historical Association, 1924; W. Freeman Galpin, "The Jerry Rescue," *New York Historical Association* 26 (1945): 19-34; Samuel J. May, *Some Recollections of Our Anti-Slavery Conflict* (Miami, Florida: Mnemosyne Publ., Co., 1959), p. 373.

29. *The Impartial Citizen*, March 20, 1850.

Chapter 4

The Abolitionist in Canada

Subsequent to looking over several Canadian cities Ward decided to settle in Toronto. He remarked that no other city had such an intense antislavery spirit save Syracuse. Without an appreciable loss of time he resumed his antislavery activities.

Ward attacked the institution of slavery, exposed all manifestations of racial discrimination, and became a renowned figure in the Anti-Slavery Society of Canada. Upon Ward's arrival in Canada Henry Bibb then editor of an antislavery newspaper out of Sandwich, Canada West, and Thomas Henning, Secretary of the Anti-Slavery Society of Canada announced their pleasure of having Ward in their country. Bibb, an escaped slave from the United States stated: "For the sake of humanity and the advancement of our cause we hope that he [Ward] may be induced to visit and lecture to our people."[1] Henning added: "Our people should feel proud of a man like S.R. Ward in Canada and we hope that he may meet with that encouragement to which his just merit entitles him."[2]

The warm welcome encouraged Ward to work diligently and elevate himself to prominent status. Soon he received an appointment as a corresponding editor of *The Aliened American* an antislavery paper published in Cleveland, Ohio. The editor of the Cleveland paper expected Ward to write a column about his experiences outside the country. But immediately following his initial editorial for the inaugural issue Ward relinquished the post. Others members on the editorial staff were fellow-abolitionists James W.C. Pennington of New York, Amos G. Beman of Connecticut, and the previously mentioned Martin R. Delany of Pittsburgh, Pennsylvania.[3]

Ward titled his only editorial to appear in *The Aliened American* "Salutation." In that piece he expressed his long-term desire to farm a plot of land. This wish to work the land may have been unrealistic as he began to do the Lord's work within forty-eight hours of his entry into Canada. As an agent for the Canadian Anti-Slavery Society he enabled himself to "do something for the moral and religious elevation"[4] of those scores of refugees fleeing from the South. Needless to say he worked arduously for the cause and his effective speaking skills went unquestioned.

A newly arrived antislavery worker in Canada Ward visited nearly every county, leading city, and town in western Canada. Observers noted that his efforts lessened a great deal of prejudice and he stimulated sympathy for the slave and the movement. As part of his responsibility Ward organized antislavery societies at Kingston, Hamilton, London, Windsor, and Grey County. Annual Reports state that Ward's meetings invariably drew large crowds of enthusiastic supporters. Furthermore, ministers who represented a variety of denominations willingly assisted him in his duties. In spite of the mob violence he encountered in the Western District Ward admitted that that ill-feeling did not reflect the overall attitude of a majority of Canadians.[5]

An optimist at heart Ward expressed good feelings following one tour through the villages of Vaughan, Markham, Pickering, and Newmarket. From his speaking tours he discovered that a surprising amount of antislavery sentiment appeared in most communities. In his speeches he illustrated his positive attitude by praising the good relationships he observed between Canadians and African Americans. He wanted to inform Canadians that many Americans were dissatisfied with American slavery. Numerous American citizens did not believe it to be a viable manifestation for any society. In fact many Anglo Americans in the United States joined with the African Americans to fight against the peculiar institution. Ward attacked openly the proslavery advocates in the United States as supporters of "despotism, and hypocrisy, practical atheism, Southern dictatorship, and recklessness of law, life and liberty."

Although Canada did not have slavery Ward did observe the existence of caste, or, as he cared to express it: "Negro-hate" or "Negrophobia." He encountered caste in two public accommodations--a hotel clerk in Hamilton, Ontario refused him a room and the staff on the cruiser Saint Lawrence refused him cabin passage. Those events did not surprise Ward since he had visited Canada a few times before this visit--however he did become deeply hurt by this show of caste. Always ready to compliment people for their good behavior Ward could also offer advice to correct injustice. As to Canadian caste he recommended universal agitation "by the press and the tongue, in church and at the polls." He suggested that efforts be introduced to rid his adopted country of this "infernal curse." Furthermore, he said: "God forgive me when I shall refuse or neglect to do my humble part in this."[6]

Caste appeared in Canada more often than not. A case in point concerned the Larwill Petition. An episode wherein Ward described Edwin Larwill the key figure behind the petition as: "By birth, a noisy, brawling, Tory politician. A man of far more consequence in his own esteem, than in that of anyone else."[7] Larwill showed himself to be a victim of xenophobia. He set out to oppose the founding of the Elgin settlement, a community designed to aid refugee blacks in their transition from slavery to freedom.[8] The infamous petition flatly disavowed the rightness or propriety of race-mixing. The measure suggested that a poll tax be levied on African Americans immigrating to Canada. Further, the petition recommended that the immigrants furnish financial security in case they become a burden to the community in which they resided. Moreover, a side-issue arose asking what the voting rights would be for the incoming blacks. The final insult put forward by Larwill and the signers of the petition asserted that the blacks were incapable of participating in civic enterprises.[9]

Ward could not allow this petition to go unnoticed. He responded immediately by penning a letter to the editor of *The Voice of the Fugitive* entitled "Canadian Negro-Hate Number Two." Aware that Larwill initiated the petition Ward said: "Jupiter could no more deny the paternity of Minerva than Edwin Larwill could deny the above (the petition) is the fruit of the base of his brain.[10] He examined the arguments in the petition and refuted each one in turn. As regards the notion of blacks settling in Canada he noted that blacks under the law of the British government "have the same right to settle upon the land, as have Irishmen or Scotchmen."[11] The petition said that too much "disgust and Negro hatred existed in Canada." Ward replied that there were benefits to be gained from integration. Very little appeared to support the statement that disgust and Negro-hatred existed. He noted from what he had seen that: "The longer whites live in the neighborhood of the blacks, the better they like them." He talked about his tour through Canada and said the charges of social unrest between blacks and whites were "utterly false." And, he declared that black people could function effectively in a public capacity. For example, he said that Toronto's sheriff had summoned numerous black voters to jury duty. They demonstrated their civic responsibility in an accepted manner. Ward ended his argument by remarking that: "In the three years since the petition was submitted to the legislature, black immigrants have come to the province and become prosperous and happy." Ward's refutation of the petition represented the best proof of its falseness.[12]

Some positive relationships did evolve from the integration of blacks and whites. But that did not eradicate the presence of Negro-hate. It created so much apprehension that the weak personality manifest in some mulattos moved them to "pass over" into white society. In order to avoid racial discrimination lighter skin African Americans would make an effort to travel in white people's circles. Ward considered this act as similar to self-destruction. Any person who "passed" actually blotted out their own heritage and their own identity. To make a decision to pass over and ignore one's past is tantamount to becoming a non-entity. Ward reflected on passing in an editorial in a Canadian paper.

> Certain of the colored inhabitants of this city of lighter complexion keep themselves aloof from the colored people, generally, and show no sort of fellow-feeling with them. They are *just a little too white to be black*, one would judge from their actions. Now, were they born in the British Empire, and had they never been identified with the cursed negro race of the United States, this snobbism would seem natural and plausible. But they are like you and me ex-slaves. The ridiculousness of this very, very small aping of aristocracy is sufficiently disgusting to be sure, but its sanction and encouragement of negro-hate, makes it especially condemnable. Such folks ought to be reckoned among our enemies. They are not friends surely.[13]

But Ward did inform the immigrant black voter who their friends were. He chided blacks for voting for a Colonel Prince, the Conservative Tory candidate in the election of 1852. The real friend of the immigrant George Brown, M.P.P. Esquire deserved their vote claimed Ward. Brown "by his pen, his press, his tongue, and his purse, had for years exhibited the most thorough, consistent and efficient friendship for the cause of the downtrodden, yet some of those (the downtrodden) voted against him." Ward wanted to help his people recognize the politicians who in his judgment were "Christlike."

Concerned over African American immigrant deportment Ward offered advice in the columns of *The Voice of the Fugitive*.

> Let poor fugitives be discouraged in the miserable habit of idling about town and village; let them be encouraged to go into the country, and become tillers and owners of the soil. Let them be aided in the acquiring of an education, let them be induced to give up alcoholic habits and beverages, and love of which is too common among us, and we should not constantly need to have letters written to friends, or foes in the United States, asking contributions in our behalf.[14]

That kind of instruction Ward believed would help to destroy the stereotypes created by the white man, that is, "blacks are ne'er-do-wells" who never will improve. From those guidelines it is apparent Ward thought the best way toward elevation for his people involved hard work, education, and cultivating acceptable social behavior. He would suggest that the incoming blacks attain these elements by "Scatteration." In other words the immigrants should scatter themselves throughout Canada so that it would be easier to assimilate into the country. People would then view the African Americans as individuals with talent instead of being thought of as a separate concentrated mass. He did not agree with the black settlers who placed themselves in isolation by their creation of a black community.

Ward would like to have seen the blacks integrate more into society because he believed the immigrants could teach the white man civility and how to live a more meaningful life. He said: "Some of their white neighbors (immigrants) need to be taught the first, basic ideas of civilization, by being near to enlightened, progressive coloured people, such as are not a few in Canada."[15] In brief, through his own suffering the slave had come to know the true meaning of love. He should, therefore, be able to teach the white man by example.

Since the runaways had undergone so much adversity Ward thought they were capable of teaching love, tolerance, and understanding to others. Although Ward's description of the escaped slave's route to freedom may seem a bit romantic it does contain real anxiety. Here he talks of the journey to Canada:

> The lonely, toiling journey; the endurance of the excitement from constant danger; the hearing the yell and howl of the bloodhound; the knowledge of close, hot pursuit; the dread of capture, and the determination not to be taken alive--all these, furnaces of trial as they are, purify and ennoble the man (sic) who has to pass through them. All these are inseparable from the ordinary incidents of the northwest passage of the fugitive: and when he (sic) reaches us, he (sic) is, first, what the raw material of nature was; and secondly, what the improving process of flight has made him (sic). Both have fitted him (sic) the more highly to appreciate, the more fully to enjoy, and the more wisely to use, that for which he (sic) came to us, for which he (sic) was willing to endure all things, for which, indeed, he (sic) would have yielded life itself--liberty.[16]

Ward glorified the slave's escape as he envisioned the slave having an "ardent and unrestrained and resistless love of liberty." Ward saw it as an ennobling and purifying act equal to the "rite of passage."[17] Here were runaways placing their manliness (sic) in what Ward referred to as "furnace of trial." They were incensed at the immoral behavior of pro-slavery men and women, and repulsed by the slave auctions, the separation of slave families, the severe floggings, the chained gangs, the murder, the incest, the fornication, and the adultery. Ward deeply believed that the fugitive represented a morally superior man or woman who exemplified purity and righteousness. These were people, Ward thought, who by virtue of their experience were qualified to educate others.

As a resident of Canada Ward continued to maintain communication with his friends in the United States. Several of his friends had written to him inquiring about the possibility of their being emigrated from America to foreign countries. Through the columns of *Frederick Douglass's Paper* Ward allayed fears of colonization or emigration. He asserted that compulsory colonization and total emigration would never occur. He referred to the past where any attempt at general emigration of the blacks had "signally failed." He cited two instances: 1) the emigration to Hayti (sic) in 1832, and, 2) the failure of an exodus to Trinidad in 1839. Those movements were both voluntary and conspicuously unsuccessful. In addition, he offered an explanation for their failure. Any class of a country's population is spread throughout the nation and mixed in with the people. It would be extremely difficult to separate these people who were perhaps related by blood.

Furthermore, blacks had not diminished in any large number from the earth. In the United States alone Ward observed that blacks increased from a half million to three million in seventy-five years. "We do not," cried Ward, "dwindle, then, under oppression, as some races do." Unlike the Jews or American Indians, blacks are constantly becoming mixed and incorporated with the people around them, he averred.

Finally, Ward explained that the destiny of a people is worked out for the better or the worst on their own native soil--even if the end result is extermination. Moreover, he believed the task of emigrating free or enslaved blacks from America entailed what is "beyond the power of mortal man."[18]

Ward's relationship with missionary societies in Canada at times proved to be strained. He opposed the activities of the Refugee Home Society, an organization established in Michigan in 1852 to aid the fugitives escaping to Canada.[19] Reverend H.D. Kitchell the local American Missionary Association (AMA) agent and Congregational minister headed the branch of the society in Amherstburg, Ontario. David Hotchkiss and an African American couple Mary and Henry Bibb shared the leadership with Kitchell.[20]

The constitution of the society proposed the purchase of fifty thousand acres of land and each family would be expected to receive twenty-five acres of farmland accompanying town lots. In three years time the society purchased some two thousand acres and sold half of it. One hundred and fifty blacks moved on to that land.[21]

Destroyed by contentiousness and greed the Refugee Home Society's in-house squabbling began when an AMA agent Mary Shadd--whose mission consisted of improving the schools--wrote to an antislavery newspaper opposing communal experimentation (blacks contained in one locale) because it retarded goals of integration.

Two issues were at the center of the controversy: 1) All of the communal experiments were subsidized by whites instead of blacks, and 2) in order to sustain the communes agents solicited funds and collected clothing in Canada, the United States, and abroad. Very few agents could solicit funds diplomatically. Most resorted to begging at churches, at antislavery society meetings, and even from house to house. The situation disturbed Ward who wrote:

> [T]he fact that it (The Refugee Home Society) sends an agent to the United States to beg money to buy land for them is of itself a representation that they (immigrants) cannot acquire such money for themselves. While the truth is, that so soon as fugitives come here, they can get work at fair wages, and so can lay by enough to buy land for themselves. NEEDING AID ONLY, allow me to repeat, NEEDING AID ONLY upon their immediate arrival, until they can get work, which in no instance that I know of is longer than three days![22]

Both Ward and Shadd criticized the begging because they predicted their would be abuses. For example, agents took twenty percent commission on the money they solicited. One of the workers granted himself twenty-five percent. After the agents took their money they purchased land with the remaining funds. Next, they gave five acres to the black settlers on the condition that they would purchase twenty additional acres. Their prices were no bargain. In some cases they were higher than the regular Canadian government fees for comparable land. On evidence of this exploitation Shadd charged the agents with malfeasance. Also, she concluded that Henry Bibb had been "the tool of Detroit whites who were mulcting the fugitives, men deliberately chosen from the more ignorant levels of the refugees so that they would ask no questions."[23]

Ward gave three reasons for disapproving of the Refugee Home Society: 1) No need existed for land buying and selling as the Canadian government already provided land, 2) the Society committed land jobbing under the name of benevolence for the immigrants, and, 3) the agents misrepresented the conditions of the refugees as they entered Canada.

Disgusted with the immoral and illegal conduct of the agents Ward refused to have his name associated with the Society. He said he could not withhold his "solemn and earnest" protest as it would be false to "my abolitionism, my love of truth, and my manhood."[24] The Society hobbled along with inner struggles, accusations, and counteraccusations. Bibb and his wife were not trusted by the fugitives. Bibb, in turn, revealed that Shadd accepted money from the Society despite her own opposition to the white men involved. Bibb eventually turned against the illegal practice but that act came too late to change the direction of the Society. Bibb died in August, 1854. His successor could not obtain permission to buy town lots. In its annual report for 1860, the Society admitted matters were not what they should have been. That understatement put it mildly since the program to aid blacks had failed miserably. That Ward educated others about the duping of the refugees attests to his deep concern for the African American immigrants in Canada.[25]

Ward continued to be concerned for the immigrants by passing on to them as much information as he could about Canada. He did this through the pages of *The Provincial Freeman* a newspaper which he owned and edited. Moreover, the paper listed Mary Shadd as publishing agent. In the inaugural issue Ward stated the paper's mission. He declared that it would be devoted to the elevation of black people. He would advocate temperance, antislavery, aid to fugitives, and the belief in the non-sectarian religion of Jesus Christ. And, when he published the political news of the day he said he would "make free comments thereon."[26]

The first issue of the *Freeman* appeared in Windsor, Ontario in March of 1853. Subsequent issues came out a year later in Toronto. Doubtless Ward's previous experience with non-paying subscribers prompted him to postpone the second issue. He informed his readers as follows: "The regular weekly issue will commence just as soon as the number of cash subscribers shall justify it."[27]

In the summer of 1855 the editor moved to Chatham taking his printing press with him. In the meantime Ward received the honor of representing the Antislavery Society of Canada in Great Britain. His instructions were: "[T]o plead the cause of the slave and let our friends know what is being done in this country for their present relief and future deliverance from bondage."[28] Or, as Ward observed the Society asked him to "[T]ake advantage of the well-known antislavery feeling of Great Britain which had intensified as a result of *Uncle Tom's Cabin*."[29] Now Ward would muster his talents and prepare to conduct a speaking tour throughout the British Isles.

Escaping from the United States to Canada the redoubtable Ward at once joined an antislavery society to inform Canadians about the evil inherent in American slavery. He traveled extensively through the provinces presenting speeches concerned with self-elevation for blacks and the racism of the whites. He helped to improve the conditions in Canada of the runaway slaves from America through the columns of various antislavery newspapers. In due course, his reputation gained for him the privilege of visiting the British Isles for the Canadian Anti-Slavery Society to further the cause of antislavery. Ward's time spent in Canada suggests that he fulfilled what he conceived to be his Christian duty to be--engaging in Christ-like work to elevate his people.

NOTES

1. *The Voice of the Fugitive*, December 19, 1851.

2. *The Voice of the Fugitive*, December 19,1851.

3. Martin E. Dann, ed., *The Black Press, 1827-1890: The Quest for National Identity* (New York: Putnam, 1971), p. 50-55.

4. Anti-Slavery Society of Canada, *First Annual Report* (Toronto, 1852), p. 15.

5. Anti-Slavery Society of Canada, *Second Annual Report* (Toronto, 1853), p. 8.

6. *The Voice of the Fugitive*, November 5, 1851.

7. *The Voice of the Fugitive*, October 21, 1852.

8. See William H. and Jane H. Pease, "Opposition to the Founding of the Elgin Settlement," *Canadian Historical Review* 38 (1957): 202-218.

9. Robin W. Winks, *The Blacks in Canada* (New Haven: Yale University Press, 1971), pp. 212-213.

10. *The Voice of the Fugitive*, September 9, 1852.

11. *The Voice of the Fugitive*, October 21, 1852.

12 *The Voice of the Fugitive*, October 21, 1852.

13. *Frederick Douglass's Paper*, December 11, 1851.

14. *The Voice of the Fugitive*, February 12,1852.

15. Ward, (1970), p. 142.

16. Ward, (1970), p. 116.

17. The "rite of passage" is referred to here for purposes of clarity. It is analogous to the fugitive slave's passing from slavery to freedom. Ward intended for his audience to see the similarity in the slave escaping to freedom and the person passing through the phase of puberty to maturity as a rite of passage.

18. *Frederick Douglass's Paper*, March 11, 1852.

19. The Refugee Home Society is discussed in Pease and Pease, Black Utopia: *Negro Communal Experiments in America* (Madison, Wisconsin, 1963), pp. 109-122, 183-184 and in Winks, (1971), pp. 204208.

20. On Bibb see Fred Landon, "Henry Bibb, A Colonizer," *Journal of Negro History* 5 (1920): 437-447.

21. Winks, (1971), p. 205.

22. *Frederick Douglass's Paper*, January 21, 1853.

23. Winks, (1971), p. 207.

24. *Frederick Douglass's Paper*, January 21, 1853.

25. Winks, (1971), p. 208.

26. *The Provincial Freeman*, March 24, 1853. A bound volume of this paper from March 24, 1853 to September 15, 1857 may be found at the University of Pennsylvania Library, Philadelphia.

27. *The Provincial Freeman*, March 24, 1853.

28. Anti-Slavery Society of Canada, *Second Annual Report* (Toronto, 1852), p. 30.

29. Ward, (1970), p. 227.

Chapter 5

The Emissary

During the peak of antislavery activity in the United States notable reformers traveled to the British Isles to elicit funds and sympathy for their cause. A host of African American abolitionists journeyed to those islands and left a deep impression on the Irish, the English, and the Scottish. Frederick Douglass traveled there as a young man and again in his later years. Other activists who journeyed to Great Britain were: James W.C. Pennington, Henry Highland Garnet, Jermain W. Loguen, and Josiah Henson.[1] Ward left Canada for England in 1853 and remained there until 1855 at which time he removed to Kingston, Jamaica in the West Indies to reside.

An exuberant and enthusiastic Ward arrived in Liverpool on April 20, 1853 anxious to begin the work of the Lord. Immediately he contacted the people to whom he had letters of recommendation. At once he began attending meetings held by the reform societies. Within a month of his arrival he appeared on the speaker's platforms at meetings of the Bible Tract Society, the Sunday School Missionary Society, and Temperance, Peace, and Anti-Slavery Societies. The pervasive atmosphere of abolitionism in Great Britain pleased him greatly.

In Scotland Ward undertook an antislavery speaking tour. He spoke at or attended meetings in Glasgow, Dundee, Edinburgh, Dalkeith, Dunfermline, Hamilton, Rothsay, Stewarttown, Cunnock, and Campbelltown. The Scottish antislavery activists impressed Ward with their sympathy for the oppressed in America.[2]

Ward spent a total of twenty days in Ireland. Later he remarked that his travels abroad taught him there were similarities among all people, regardless of their national origin. He observed that while the

Irish were not technically enslaved their association with the established ruling powers came close to the master-slave relationship of American blacks. The Irish peasants were ensnared in conditions where their basic economic needs were far below the marginal. Oppression, said Ward, came in many forms. He found the poorer sections of New York City, Boston, and Philadelphia not as physically and morally decayed as some places he viewed in Ireland. In some cases the Irish were worse off than American blacks. "Never did I see such degradation as abounds not only in the towns, but in the rural districts of Ireland."[3]

Ward lamented the fact that blacks and Irish were at odds. The Irish immigrant in America would discriminate against the African American who could claim the United States as his or her native land. Ward considered the differences as shameful since both people had much in common. That is to say, "The wit, warmth and enthusiasm--the capacity to imitate, to improve, and to endure--the cheerfulness, bravery and love of religion--said to be peculiar to the Celt, are well-known characteristics of the Negro."[4]

Regarding Ward's visit to Wales he discovered that a correct social and moral life will elevate a class of people. He learned that Wales had a low crime rate, a lack of prostitution, a minimum of drunkards, an absence of beggars, and a quiet, undisturbed mood in the towns and villages. Moreover, the people on the streets of Wales appeared to be well behaved and civil. He attributed the Calvinist Methodist Church of that country responsible for the high moral conduct and proper deportment in the people.[5]

In an attempt to illustrate that blacks as well as whites are equal among all classes Ward alluded several times to his being in the company of the nobility of England. He dedicated his autobiography to his friend the Duchess of Sutherland and he mentioned being invited many times to the homes of Lords and Ladies. While on his speaking tours he spent much time in the company of "people in high station in life." Ward expressed satisfaction as he disproved the myth that he and his people could not consort with those persons in an elevated social position. Although he recognized that these people of higher rank were not any different from other classes he did observe that among the more sophisticated of society caste, prejudice, and discrimination were at a minimum.

As to Ward's mission to go to England to solicit funds for the Canadian Anti-Slavery Society it should be noted that he collected twelve hundred pounds sterling while on tour. At one point "L400 of this sum has been sent out to Canada, a portion of which has been devoted to the payment of Mr. Ward's expenses, a part to the aiding of the Fugitives, and the balance is at interest in the Bank at the call of the Treasurer."[6]

Unfortunately some of Ward's transactions reveal a tinge of dishonesty. Prior to leaving England he had been given fifty acres of land in the parish of Saint George, Jamaica, West Indies by a Quaker, John Candler of Chelmsford. When he prepared to visit his new holdings Ward became involved in financial negotiations with William Baynham, a London tradesman. Baynham loaned Ward one hundred forty pounds. Apparently Ward assured Baynham that he had five thousand pounds back in Toronto. In addition, Ward persuaded Baynham to sell his business and emigrate to Canada. Arrangements were made for the two to meet in Toronto for repayment of the debt. Baynham left on a sailing ship with Ward following on a steamship. Ward's ship however sailed to Jamaica, West Indies.

Baynham arrived in Canada only to discover that Ward had not returned to Toronto to repay his debt. The Canadian Anti-Slavery Society gave temporary relief to Baynham and his family. In the meantime Baynham queried British abolitionists in London to find out if Ward had been in the habit of representing himself as a man of property. Unfortunately the London Committee's reply has not been preserved. But Henning's response to the missing reply is informative. Apparently the London people confirmed what had happened between Baynham and Ward. Henning regretted the painful circumstances created by Ward. The Canadian Anti-Slavery Society offered no further explanation or reactions to the episode. Ironically Ward's autobiography had just appeared on the market and received favorable reviews. This situation may have caused suppression of any possible publicity about the event.[7] In any case Ward sailed to Jamaica in 1855 to occupy the land given to him by the Quaker John Candler.

Ward's background does not reveal any criminal wrongdoing. And, no signs exist that show him as being a confidence man. A hard worker, a decent family man, and a God-fearing individual it is unfathomable that he would be capable of such an act. It is a mystery why he would do such a thing since he enjoyed his association with the people of high station while in Britain.

One explanation does come to mind. The gardening he did with his father as a child made a deep impression on him and he regularly made references to farming and living in the country away from city life. He recommended to blacks that they move to the country and take up farming, he held a deep affection for the rolling hills, the scenic beauty of the countryside, and, on occasion he threatened to purchase some land and become a farmer. Perhaps he became so disenchanted with the progress of the antislavery movement that he decided to farm his land in Jamaica. But events seemed to dictate Ward's activities.

Ward traveled to Jamaica as the "representative of some Christian organization; but whether for the purpose of direct religious work or for business, is not certain."[8] In Kingston, Jamaica he accepted the pastorate of a group of dissidents from Kingston's Baptist Church. His meetings were held at thirty-four Hanover Street, and he resided on the premises.[9] He remained pastor of the church until 1860. Differences of opinion arose between Ward and his congregation; the end result witnessed Ward's resignation. After the Kingston experience Ward settled on some property in Saint Thomas-in-the-East. He took up his lifelong dream of farming but ill health prevented him from realizing his wish. Evidently Ward ended his days in abject poverty in 1866. He was survived by a married son who had three daughters all of whom were alive and residents of Kingston in 1933. It is unclear as to the whereabouts of his wife when Ward died.[10]

Inasmuch as Ward had become a controversial figure there were many rumors about his activities. Two years after leaving Great Britain his name appeared in a New York City Newspaper. An item in the paper titled, "A Fugitive Slave Sent to Van Diemen's Island," declared Ward committed an offense in Jamaica, was sent to prison, and his wardrobe returned to his family in Canada.[11] A month later there appeared another news item about Ward. The piece read as follows: "The report that Rev. Samuel R. Ward, the black preacher, has been sent to a penal colony for forgery, is contradicted. He is preaching with great success in Jamaica, West Indies, and has sent for his family."[12] In the short time Ward lived in Kingston he exercised "A powerful influence over the black and coloured population." He worked his way to become head of a political party wherein he controlled local elections.[13]

Ward observed the deplorable conditions of the black people in Jamaica and began at once to work for their improvement. At special meetings he protested the slave trade, he favored African American immigration to Jamaica, and he frowned upon the mulatto leadership associated with the Morant Bay Rebellion. Those problems are discussed subsequently.

In February of 1857 Ward participated in a meeting convened to discuss the slave trade in Jamaica. "Several resolutions were passed and supported by others," to halt the trading in human beings. Ward's contribution consisted of reminding his auditors that the Spanish had been paid four hundred thousand pounds to stop their slave trade but they continued to practice it in any event.[14]

At another meeting Ward addressed the matter of providing asylum for the "expelled free men and women of America."[15] He recommended to the committee in charge of the American Immigration Plan that they offer educational opportunities to the incoming black Americans. If an inducement of this kind were not offered to them, they would be discouraged from residing in Jamaica. If the offer were rendered it must be complied with faithfully. In fact he proposed that the Jamaican Immigration Act be amended to provide for the education of all children who immigrate to the island.[16] Ward explained his thoughts on immigration in the following excerpt from a seconding speech:

> That this island would be greatly benefited by the accession to the population of a portion of their American brethren, and there is every reason to believe that from the excellence of the climate, the rich and varied productions of the soil, the abundance of unoccupied land, and its social and political condition (which opens to all equally every avenue to the attainment of a comfortable and respectable position in life, under free institutions, and under letters of naturalization obtained without cost, conferring the equal rights and privileges of British subjects), the exchange of country would be beneficial; and this meeting hails with pleasure the prospect of such an occasion, and the life and energy which it would impart to every interest.[17]

In that excerpt we see Ward's optimism carried to the extreme. The state of the economy in Jamaica favored the aristocracy while poverty among the poor and black steadily increased. Taxes soared, widespread hunger existed, and very few blacks could vote. Black immigrants in the 1850's lived in abject poverty and squalid conditions. The increased immigration led the workers to demand higher wages, request an opportunity to own land, and seek generally improved living and working conditions.[18]

Consequently the Morant Bay Rebellion occurred in October, 1865 because of the conditions just described. In the rebellion an English magistrate and eighteen white persons were slain by rebels. Moved by fear and contempt the white governor of the island summarily quelled the uprising with all of the military power he could muster. Over four hundred blacks were shot, a thousand homes were burned to the ground, and many insurgents mercilessly flogged.[19]

A year later Ward commented on the events of the rebellion. He condemned the uprising as "the treasonable and seditious teachings" of George William Gordon, the leader of the revolt who was hanged. Ward sided with the Jamaican government forces and agreed with the severity "which was impossible to blunt" during the riots. Ward concurred with the strong arm of repression used by the Governor Edward John Eyre who would receive instructions to return to England at a later date. Subsequently stringent security measures were implemented in the governance of the island .[20]

Disappointed over the rebel leaders Ward criticized their manipulation of black people.

> In Saint Anne, Saint Dorothy, Vere, Kingston, Saint Thomas-in-the-East; in Parliament, by letters, placards, harangues, by means of various agents and subagents, by political stratagems, vestry broils, party bickerings, and secret cabals; by specious misrepresentations and downright lies, all designed and tending to unsettle the minds of the lower classes, and to teach them to disregard and undervalue the authorities of the land from the Governor down to their employers.[21]

Ward reported that the tone of certain newspapers greatly aided Gordon's cause. Additionally, Ward noted that a general laxity of men in authority allowed Gordon's activities to go unquestioned and even refuted. Ward believed that if Gordon's movement "of which he was the Napoleon" had been questioned, he would not have succeeded. Ward understood that if the "lower classes" were left alone "and had nothing been said or done to unsettle and excite them" then Jamaica would not have had the horrendous blood bath.

The entire episode enraged Ward because of the effect on the black man's character. This is how he responded

> Everybody knows that the negro is not judged by the same rule that is applied to other men (sic). Nobody stigmatizes all Irishmen (sic) because of the Fenian scheme. Nobody

> blames all Americans because of the Southern rebellion. Fenians and their sympathizers are blamed for Fenianism, and they only. Southern rebels and their active coadjutors are held responsible for rebellion and no one else. But the whole mass of negroes are too commonly classed and generalized, with any portion who do wrong. To protest against this, were needless in any other cases, for the simple reason that some people will not see any good in the negro.[22]

Furthermore, Ward complained that so many blacks were led into the rebellion and made subordinates and "cat's paws to a mulatto and his confreres."

Ward held an intense dislike for the mulatto leader because he did not think Gordon provided the correct social and moral elevation for his people. He stated that Gordon did not represent blacks. Ward looked to all blacks regardless of their skin color to be proud of their background. He did not think Gordon held an interest in black pride. He thought that Gordon had intended on "A general massacre, a new distribution of property, among the rebel chiefs and their retainers, and the elevation of Mr. G.W. Gordon to the seat of supreme authority. To effect these objects no man of any race, color, or position, who stood in the way, was to be spared."[23]

Similar in his thinking to other black leaders of the day Ward encouraged an ethnocentricity or black pride among his African American brothers and sisters. He intended to illustrate that blacks can be an imaginative and creative social force in a society. Ward's criticism embodied the idea that blacks could profit more from social, moral, and political uplift than by choosing to follow an insurgent mulatto leader who intended on setting up a despotic rule. Apparently Ward did not participate in the uprising but he did function as a critical bystander. Unfortunately the historical records on Ward's activities come to an abrupt halt at this juncture. Archives at the Jamaican Institute in Kingston and governmental records at Spanish Town contain nothing on Ward after 1866. However, the little we have been able to uncover reveals that Ward involved himself in social and moral reform and considered it as labor of the first order. We know that he continued to look for ways and means to elevate his people for most of his time in Jamaica.

To summarize then: Born in slavery on the Eastern Shore of Maryland on October 17, 1817 Samuel Ringgold Ward and his parents escaped to the free northern states in 1820. Ward grew up in New Jersey and New York City, attended the New York African Free-School which significantly affected his adult life as an abolitionist speaker. As a young man he worked in New York City for small business owners who were sympathetic to the cause of freedom. Fortunately he was able to participate in antislavery activities with the new breed of black militants who emerged in the 1830's and 1840's. Young Samuel became deeply influenced by the reform mood that emphasized an involvement in social and moral reform.

At twenty-one years of age Ward became an antislavery agent for the American Anti-Slavery Society. He labored for the society for a short time until he assumed the pastorate of an all-white congregation in South Butler, New York. In South Butler Ward tested some of his ideas and discovered that he had exceptional powers in articulating his beliefs. Subsequent to his tenure in South Butler Ward moved to Geneva, New York to care for an illness of the throat. After a short time in Geneva he traveled to Cortlandville, New York to pastor the local Congregational Church. In Cortlandville Ward witnessed the full flowering of his inner talents. His education, his family background, his association with fellow abolitionists, and his devotion to the life of Christ crystallized to the extent that Ward rendered a significant contribution to the antislavery movement in Central New York. There he continued to interrelate with a variety of reformers renowned for their Christian Abolitionism. Soon other antislavery activities concerned with the Fugitive Slave Bill occupied Ward's time.

Unable to resist taking part in the rescuing of the fugitive Slave Jerry in Syracuse, New York Ward assisted by helping to saw off Jerry's leg irons. Moreover, Ward presented a stirring public address outside of the courthouse that held Jerry. The speech may have helped to stimulate the crowd of reformers to act. Involvement in the Jerry Rescue caused Ward to move to Canada to escape federal prosecution. In Canada he became an agent for the Canadian Anti-Slavery Society and devoted much time informing the citizens about the evils of racism and American slavery. In time Ward received instructions from the Canadian Anti-Slavery Society to travel to Great Britain to solicit funds and moral support for the cause. In London he fell from the heights of popularity when he borrowed a large sum of money and failed to pay it back.

From Great Britain Ward sailed to Jamaica, West Indies to presumably farm some land that had been presented to him as a gift.

In Jamaica he participated in politics and he pastored a church. He protested vehemently against the exploitation practiced by the mulatto leaders on the "lower class" blacks. As far as can be ascertained Ward died in abject poverty in Jamaica in 1866 regardless of some unsubstantiated rumors that appeared in the New York City papers. Ward's entire life exemplified that of a dedicated servant to the poor and the oppressed. Although he marred his life by one disreputable incident he threw himself totally into the elevation of black men and women.

NOTES

1. Quarles, (1969), p. 133.
2. Quarles, (1969), p. 228-230.
3. Quarles, (1969), p. 244-259.
4. Quarles, (1969), p. 260-265.
5. Quarles, (1969), p. 266.
6. *Frederick Douglass's Paper*, July 14, 1854.
7. See Alexander L. Murray, "Canada and the Anglo-American Anti-Slavery Movement: A Study in International Philanthropy," unpublished diss., Ph.D. (University of Pennsylvania, 1960), pp. 275-277.
8. *The Institute of Jamaica Archives*, Jamaica, West Indies, Frank Cundall to George W. Forbes, Esquire, at West End Branch Public Library, Boston, Massachusetts, August 10, 1909.
9. The site of the church where Ward pastored is now in the heart of the bordello district. Research undertaken by writer, Summer, 1973.
10. Frank Cundall, long-time historian of the Institute of Jamaica attributes this information to "presumably trustworthy sources." See *Institute of Jamaica Archives*, Cundall to Honorable Colonial Secretary, December 10, 1933.
11. *The New York Tribune*, March 7, 1857.
12. *The New York Tribune*, April 7, 1857.
13. *Institute of Jamaica Archives*, Cundall to Honorable Colonial Secretary, December 10, 1933.
14. *The Daily Advertiser and Lawton's Commercial Gazette*, February 13, 1857. This paper is on hand at the Institute of Jamaica, Kingston, Jamaica, W.I.
15. *The Falmouth Post and Jamaica General Advertiser*, May 4, 1857. paper on hand at the Institute of Jamaica, Kingston, W.I.
16. *The Falmouth Post and Jamaica General Advertiser*, May 7, 1858.
17. *The Falmouth Post and Jamaica General Advertiser*, May 4, 1858.
18. John Hope Franklin, *From Slavery to Freedom* fourth edition (New York: Alfred A. Knopf, 1974), Chapter IV. Also see: *Encyclopaedia Brittanica* 12 (Chicago, 1969): 851-852.
19. Samuel Ringgold Ward, *Reflections Upon the Gordon Rebellion*, Jamaica, W.I., 1866 (publisher unknown). Copy on hand at

Department of Rare Books and Special Collections, The University of Michigan, University Library, Ann Arbor, Michigan 48109.

20. Ward, (1866).
21. Ward, (1866).
22. Ward, (1866).
23. Ward, (1866).

Introduction to Part Two

Part two of this book is devoted to a rhetorical criticism of the written and spoken extant materials of the Reverend Mister Samuel Ringgold Ward. This section includes five chapters three of which use the classical canons of rhetoric to analyze the discourses. The ancients divided the canons of rhetoric into five areas, that is, invention (the gathering of the speaker's materials), arrangement (the proper placement of those materials), memory (the keeping in the speaker's mind of those materials), style (the language used by the speaker) and delivery (the use of the face, the body, and the voice by the speaker). Two chapters conclude the volume by discussing the effectiveness of Ward's speaking and the findings of the study.

A distinction between the biographical discussion in Part One and the rhetorical criticism in Part Two is necessary at this point. Frederick Marcham in his article distinguishes clearly between speech studies and historical studies. "The student of speech," he observed, "has benefited by the historian's ability to describe the influence, if any, of the speech on the course of affairs."[1] On the other hand, he noted: "The historian has benefited by the ability of the student of speech to present the speech to us in its most exact form and to criticize it as a work of art."[2]

Also, Ernest Bormann has recognized the difference between historical research and speech criticism noting that: "The critic's focus on artistry is the major difference between the critical and the historical method. the critic, to do his (sic) job fully, must make judgments about the work he (sic) is criticizing."[3] Bormann went on:

> To make such evaluations, the critic must establish standards of excellence. The standards should have a certain universality and permanence. The critic is aware of the historical context in which the play or speech was produced, but whether a play was written in three days or three years or

> whether it was the playwright's first successful play or last, the critic's judgment may still be based on the merit of the work.[4]

Bormann ended his comments by stating that: "The establishment of artistic standards for appreciating rhetoric or drama or interpretation of for judging the play, speech, novel or poem is the main difference between the function of the critic and the historian."[5] In brief the application of appropriate analytical tools can help the rhetorical critic to realize certain perspectives from the public discourse that would be lost to others.

This rhetorical analysis follows the guidelines set forth in the *Rhetorica Ad Herrenium*. In that book it is asserted that: "The task of the public speaker is to secure as far as possible the agreement of his (sic) hearers."[6] That is, the speaker is to direct his or her efforts at persuading the audience to concur with the proposition inherent in the discourse. The achievement of such a goal Cicero believed required skill in the five canons of rhetoric mentioned above.[7] This rhetorical analysis will examine each of the components of the canons of rhetoric with the aid of principles and precepts from the writings of Cicero and Aristotle.[8] More, I will attempt to ascertain the degree of the speaker's effectiveness as well as describe Ward's theory of rhetoric. It is my contention that Ward took advantage of the classical canons of rhetoric and put them to excellent use in persuading his audiences.

Whereas Ward adhered to the Ciceronian theory of rhetoric he also aligned himself with other classical theorists. For example, he appeared to respond to the Aristotlean definition of rhetoric, that is, "the faculty of observing in any given case the available means of persuasion."[9] Paul Ried's discussion of classical theories can aid in clarifying the relationship between Aristotle and Cicero:

> While there are substantial differences between the rhetorics of Aristotle and Cicero, one of the beliefs they shared was the view of rhetoric which hypothesized a popular audience and a responsible speaker. The speaker is distinctive in that he (sic) employs techniques to bring to the masses a clear, well-reasoned, and effective idea. Their rhetorics, then, dealt with the "authorship" of the speaker, his invention, disposition, elocution, memory, and action. They further regarded the topics of commonplace as residual elements of an education which speakers could carry with them and employ regardless

> of audience, occasion, and time. the speaker was conceived of as removed from, but responsible for his audience. His ethic was a recognition of this responsibility and his credibility depended on it.[10]

It is important to keep in mind then, the analytical tools of the rhetorical critic. An analysis of Ward's extant works will suggest that when he wrote or spoke he exploited many of the resources at his command. It should be mentioned that inasmuch as the content of the editorials in Ward's newspaper *The Impartial Citizen* replicated his speech topics we can assume that not much difference existed between the two. Presumably major content changes were not rendered from the written word to the spoken word.

Lastly it must be remembered that the initial contention of this study is that Ward's Christology remained basic to his participation in social and moral reform. Consequently the Reverend Mister Samuel Ringgold Ward understood that the employment of classical rhetoric could be a valuable means by which he would disseminate the gospel of Jesus Christ to his audiences.

NOTES

1. Frederick George Marcham, "History and Speech Collaborative Studies, Present and Future," *The Quarterly Journal of Speech* 35 (1949): 285.

2. Marcham, (1949).

3. Ernest G. Bormann, *Theory and Research in the Communicative Arts* (New York: Holt, Rinehart & Winston, 1965), p. 229.

4. Bormann, (1965).

5. Bormann, (1965).

6 Marcus Tullius Cicero, *Rhetorica Ad Herrenium*, trans. Harry Caplan (Cambridge, Massachusetts: Harvard University Press, 1954), p.5.

7. Caplan (1954).

8. Caplan, (1954), p. 7.

9. Aristotle, *Rhetoric and Poetics* trans. W. Rhys Roberts and Ingram Bywater (New York: Random House, Inc., 1954), p. 24.

10. Paul E. Ried, "A Brief Historical Orientation to Speech Communication Models," (unpublished monograph) (1975) Syracuse University.

Chapter 6

Rhetorical Development

As a young man Ward recognized the need to perfect his ability as a public speaker. He witnessed that his contemporaries received many benefits as a result of their command of language. The need to perfect communication skills became more and more evident as his career as an abolitionist advanced. His self confidence began to develop in his student days and continued to grow into his adulthood. Years later he reminisced how early training helped him: "In July, 1837, I was selected to deliver an oration before a Literary Society of which I was a member. It was my first attempt at public speaking."[1] That literary society proved vital in Ward's speech training. Typically these early nineteenth century literary societies provided much of the basic training available to young people. In the words of historian Dorothy Porter:

> Some of the expressed reasons for the organization of these institutions were the stimulation of reading and the spreading of useful knowledge by providing libraries and reading rooms, the encouragement of expressed literary efforts by providing audiences as critics and channels of publication for training of future orators and leaders by means of debates.[2]

The efforts of these societies were rewarded when blacks who lacked education became knowledgeable not only on public issues but public speaking as well. In order to elevate their condition blacks were taught to read. And, as in Ward's case many engaged in debate and were taught the skills of public discourse. "The lecture platform of these societies," observed Porter "was the workshop and preparatory school for many of the Negro antislavery lecturers who later won fame in America and England as public speakers."[3] To support this fact Ward explained that as a result of his experience in the literary society he disciplined himself first to speak in private homes and then in public places until he became accustomed to the sound of his own voice "and a little skilled in the handling of the subject, receiving encouragement from one friend and another."[4]

During the period of his early training Ward worked for David Ruggles who "was probably the earliest Negro book collector." Ruggles maintained "a circulating library and made available to many readers antislavery and colonization publications."[5] In all probability Ward strengthened his education by having access to Ruggles's private library.

Ward familiarized himself with public issues by engaging in debates, by keeping apprised of current events, by reading antislavery journals and newspapers, and by observing the orations of his fellow abolitionists. And, as pastor to the congregation in South Butler and in Cortlandville he had ample opportunity to refine his skills.

It is helpful to visualize Ward on an antislavery speaking tour if we are to appreciate the context in which he approached the speech situation. More than likely he wore his cleric's suit with a white shirt and a black string tie as he hustled his horse and carriage over the plank roads or dirt turnpikes in upstate New York. It is probable that he stopped in a town or village to deliver a pre-arranged speech in a church, a town hall, or a schoolhouse. Ordinarily the length of his speeches would be an hour or an hour and a half. Some of the topics he addressed were: "Temperance," "Religious Duties of Black Men," "Character," "Antislavery," or "The Second Advent."

At the end of Ward's speech he solicited subscriptions for his paper *The Impartial Citizen* and then possibly he would be invited to attend a tea or social gathering at one of the homes in the village. A gregarious person Ward took delight in these gatherings after traveling alone on the road. On occasion he would dine with friends sometimes staying overnight with the local clergy. Otherwise he would continue on to his next speaking engagement.

Ward arranged a very ambitious and rigorous schedule for one speaking tour. It happened that he assigned himself nine speaking events in nine towns within ten days. Often he traveled in severe winter weather which occasionally affected his health. For example at one point in his travels he said: "I am now suffering from a severe cold, that it is with difficulty that I sit up long enough to write," he reported in October, 1849. On that same trip he started from

Sherburne, New York but was detained due to a slight accident involving his horse and harness. Once on the road however he encountered one of the severest storms he had ever seen. Then, as he drove the forty-six miles from Cazenovia to Milan in Cayuga County he found pleasure in seeing that despite the blizzard fifty men and a dozen women braved the elements to attend his lecture. Injecting a tone of levity into the situation he remarked that he "never saw such a set of water-proof reformers."[6] On another occasion after driving the forty miles of plank roads between Syracuse and Oswego Ward commented: "[T]he toll gates are pretty thick, but the rest is a good one and I have my team travel over it in three and half hours."[7] Such a demanding schedule sometimes led Ward to complain:

> In November, 1839, I made my debut as a lecturer. It cost me a great deal of effort and self-denial. My youthful wife and my infant boy I must leave, to go hundreds of miles, travelling (sic) in all weathers, meeting all sorts of people, and in the majority of instances denied the ordinary courtesies of civilized life. I went forth, and from that day to this I have never been able to see this travelling (sic), homeless, part of the work in any other light than a cross. No place can be a substitute for home.[8]

However, from another perspective travel had its compensations. Ward received great respect from the reformers he met on the road and the fellow clergy who fed and lodged him. The recipient of numerous invitations to teas he invariably became the focus of much attention. And, doubtless the more curious would be drawn to him at social gatherings to inquire about the latest developments in the movement. No doubt this conviviality lessened the hardships of the journey.

Now that we have looked at Ward on the antislavery speaking circuit it would be valuable to examine the many elements that contributed to the creation of Ward's theory of rhetoric. It is necessary to begin with invention, that is, the forms of appeal inherent in Ward's public discourses. Subordinate to invention are the ethical, emotional, and logical forms of appeal used by the orator. As this chapter proceeds we will analyze the invention of Ward as well as criticize two of Ward's orations.

As Ward toured upstate New York, and later, Canada in his role as a Christian abolitionist each speech evidenced characteristics which stemmed from his own peculiar approach to the process of invention.[9]

Ward usually established his credibility by expressing his good intentions as an antislavery laborer, revealing his intelligence by his word choice in his orations, and demonstrating his integrity by his actions. As regards his good intentions he exclaimed that he would be: "[T]he friend of the poor Man (sic), north and south, white and black, at home and abroad."[10] Once more he expressed his good intentions:

> As an humble advocate of antislavery principles, it was my duty, under the guidance of the great chiefs of the cause, to drag out to the light secret plots and mischievous though hidden machinations of the slave power--to preach the gospel of deliverance to the captives--and to aid, counsel and encourage, my own, the black people, in what was needed in their peculiar circumstances.[11]

Ward never failed to establish his good will and his devotion to the oppressed.

Members of the Canadian Anti-Slavery Society expressed their appreciation for Ward's dedication at one of their meetings. According to one account a member said: "The indefatigable exertions of Mr. Ward have been very successful. His eloquence as a speaker has rendered him very popular, and has done much to weaken the prejudice that exists against persons of color even in Canada."[12]

That Ward would say the following about human bondage: "[I]n the name of the insulted majesty of High Heaven, I protest with all my soul, against this damnable heresy,"[13] attests to the intensity of his dislike for slavery. Anger at such a high pitch served to strengthen his determination to fight for black freedom.

To an angry mob in Syracuse, New York Ward expressed dedication to his black brethren by saying that the United States claimed to be a democracy, yet it captured and enslaved black people.[14] Again he displayed his devotion to black people when prior to sailing to the West Indies he asserted: "It may be that our Heavenly Father will permit me to be of some service to my people in that island."[15] His good will and intentions of supporting his people through Christ-like labor were unmistakable in his rhetoric.

Ward established his intelligence as an orator by his erudition, that is, his evident training in the classics, and his apparent knowledge of literature. Regularly in his speeches he quoted from famous personages. He made reference to Alexander Pope's claim that "White and black soften the blend in so many thousand ways, that it is neither white nor black."[16] He discussed proudly many famous black persons in history--he mentioned Cyprian, Tertullian, Euclid, and Terence.[17] He displayed his knowledge of history when he referred to the Irish patriots Curran, Emmett, O'Connell, O'Brien, and Barrington[18] He quoted the liberal and compassionate poet John Greenleaf Whittier: "Freedom, hand in hand, with labour, Walketh, strong and brave; While, on the brow of his neighbor, No man Writeth-Slave."[19]

His knowledge impressed his listeners on one occasion when he identified with Thomas Jefferson. It so happened that he disagreed with suffragist Lucretia Mott and explained that: "We believe with Jefferson, that errors of opinion may safely be tolerated, if reason be left free to combat them."[20] He relied on Jefferson again in referring to a runaway slave who fled to Canada. He proclaimed that the fugitive did not emulate the men "more apt to bear evils than to put themselves to the peril and trouble of getting rid of them."[21]

Ward appeared well bred as he frequently employed the Latin phrase. When he claimed his wife forever present in spirit as he traveled on the speaking circuit he adverted to her as a *vade mecum.*[22] He said the church's maltreatment of black people appeared to be a *sine qua non.*[23] He found the phrase *in forma* convenient many times for a particular occasion.[24] In describing a group of New York abolitionists he used the idiom *et id omne genus.*[25] No doubt he found the use of Latin phrases impressed his audiences thus giving the lie to the widely held idea of black uneducability.

Ward showed his first-rate mind even more when he shared with his audiences his familiarity with the Bible. For example, he quoted from Isaiah as he excoriated the unrighteous: "To break the yoke and let the oppressed go free." Following the Gordon Rebellion in Jamaica he wished for a period to arrive on earth when "what is written in the first Book of Chronicles, 4th Chapter, 40th verse will be true now, and hereafter, as it was then. 'The land was wide (i.e., well cultivated) and quiet and peaceable, for they of Ham had dwelt there of old.'" He criticized the church for its discriminating "Negro pews" and quoted Christ as saying: "All ye are brethren." He called the peculiar institution of slavery a mammonocracy, and alluded to the slaveowner's greed by saying: "Lay not up for yourselves treasures on earth."

We have looked at Ward's good will and intelligence. Let us now examine his integrity. Ranked among men of distinction journalists knew Ward as a "distinguished colored orator."[26] The editor Martin R. Delany--mentioned earlier--conceptualized Ward's place in the eyes of his contemporaries by recalling that "Governor Seward said that he 'never heard true eloquence until he heard Samuel R. Ward speak.'"[27] Delany continued to say that Horace Greeley, New York City editor and political leader, declared that "Capt. Rynders and Dr. Grant, the famous Democratic leaders of the Infidel Club of Tammany Hall, compared with (Ward) are but second-rate monkeys."[28] Also, Delany remembered the eloquence of Ward "at the great Free Soil Convention at Buffalo, in 1848, in the midst of assembled thousands--lawyers, judges, politicians, members of Congress and Senators."[29]

Ward then, established his credibility (ethical appeal) by way of his good intentions, his intelligence, and his integrity. We can now examine his ability to stir the emotions (emotional appeal) in his audiences. Ward's emotional appeals were inextricably woven into the subject matter of his speeches. To be sure he did not arouse the emotions of his listeners without foundation. He inspired audiences with his genuineness and his unpretentiousness. For example, he spoke to the idea of justice for everyone: "I go for Equal Rights; the Equal Rights of *all men*--not as a mere abstract, speculative theory, but as a great practical idea, to be realized in the workings, and recognized as the subject, and aim of Civil Government."[30] He worked at winning over the audience by telling them he would labor for abolitionism, "whether in the editorial chair, in the pulpit, on the platform, pleading for this cause or that."[31] He made an appeal to amity and to pride by instructing African Americans to be true to themselves and each other. He said to be above vice and crime is the way to gain improved conditions.[32]

Samuel J. May, noted minister-abolitionist described Ward's emotional remarks at one event as "very spirited" and recalled Ward saying he would "make the most violent resistance to any attempt that might be made to re-enslave them (fugitives). They would have their liberty or die in its defense."[33] Ward could stir the passions quickly as when he stated: "[H]ad you worn a colored skin from October 1817 to June, 1840, as I have, in this pseudo-Republic, you would have seen through a very different medium."[34]

In reference to the Fugitive Slave Bill the subject invariably stimulated highly passionate remarks from Ward:

> Now, this bill strips us of all manner of protection, by the writ of *habeus corpus*, by jury trial, or by any other process known to the laws of civilized nature, that are known as safeguards around personal liberty. But while it does this, it throws us

> back upon the natural and inalienable rights of self-defense--self-protection. It solemnly refers to each of us, individually, the question, whether we will submit to being enslaved by the hyenas which this law creates and encourages, or whether we will protect ourselves, even if in so doing, we have to peril our lives and more *than peril the useless and devilish carcasses of negro-catchers*. It gives us that alternative of dying freemen, or living slaves. Let the men who execute this bill beware. Let them know that the business of catching slaves, or kidnapping freemen, is an open warfare upon the rights and liberties of the black men of the North. Let them know to enlist in that warfare is present, certain, inevitable death and damnation. Let us teach them, that none should engage in this business, but those who are ready to be offered up on the polluted altar of accursed slavery.[35]

The tone communicated in that excerpt reflects the unrestrained and inflammatory appeal that Ward could convey to arouse the emotions.

Specific acts of brutality that he detailed in his public discourses would stir the emotions. He informed a Canadian audience of the terrible cruelty in slavery. He talked of the "human business of wielding the driver's whip over the backs, and burying the driver's lash into the naked and quivering flesh of helpless men and women."[36]

To jostle the feelings of his listeners Ward mixed religion with compassion. In attempting to comfort his people he said: "Our abiding place is here; and our Saviour in a *day to come*, will arise for the sighing of the poor and the crying of the needy, and set him against him that puffeth at him."[37] He awoke sentiments by a discussion of Jesus Christ. He told his auditors that his own understanding of Christology is that men and women engaged in Christ's work is a guarantee of black liberation. He would remind his people of what Christ said: "I am the way." As Christians we are aware of the poor among us. Thus, just as Christ showed his compassion toward the meek so must the Christian. He hoped for a time to arrive when a Christian could say: "Let there be no strife, pray thee, between thee and me, and between thy herdman and my herdman, for we be brethren."

Ward often made use of the emotional narration such as the time he related a story he had been told in Wales. He met a Welsh family with a sick child whose mother told Ward that in the midst of severe pain, her sick little boy would say: "Mamma, I ought not to complain so. How much did Jesus suffer for me?"[38] Ward commented that he ceased complaining after he learned of that child's situation.

Ward played on the emotions of his listeners by his use of wit and sarcasm. For example, after speaking to an audience of between four and five hundred he remarked that more people would have attended had they known that a black man was to speak. "Supposing me to be *nothing but a white man*, they did not take pains to attend, Well."[39] Once again he poked fun at the whites who believed blacks to be intellectually inferior. He continued to ease the burden of his antislavery labors when he humorously referred to a substantial collection of subscription funds he had solicited for his paper. He alluded to the politicians's corrupt ways by saying with this kind of money he "could afford to stay out of Congress."[40]

Sarcasm surfaced in Ward's rhetoric at times. He talked of his alleged liberal friends who thought of him as a "pretty good coin to go to meeting with but not worth a groat to go to mill or market with."[41] In other words, Ward felt that some whites were embarrassed to be in public with him. Further, he remembered that in Sunday School he had been taught that he would be white in Heaven and his soul would be as white as anyone else's. He countered that racist thought by noting that if he judged white in Heaven by what he had seen of "white" on earth then he wished to be excused from any complexional change whatever.[42] In his use of emotional appeal then, Ward understood the kind of language that made an audience respond.

Perhaps the most singularly persuasive element of Ward's rhetoric emerged in his use of logic (logical appeal). His rhetoric displays a remarkable ability to think out, argue, prove, or disprove a position. His logic appeared flawless and well supported. Invariably he went to the center of an issue in order to consider the basic problem first. On the issue of slavery, for example, he said: "But men had been obliged to listen to the discussion of the question (slavery) in the halls of Congress during last winter--not because they had willed it, but because there was a God in Israel. That was a most significant indication that the discussion could not be prevented."[43] In short, slavery represented a sin against God and men and women. Inasmuch as slavery bore that definition he said it became inevitable that it would be debated in Congress.

Ward's logic dominated again as he offered a basic definition of liberty and slavery in one of his public discourses:

What was the grand issue? What was the reason for the mobs

> and conflagrations and assassinations of other years? The offense was in believing that the Declaration of Independence was a matter of fact and not a fiction. That was the only issue; and the great question whether the principles of the Declaration of Independence are to be transmitted to future generations was not unsettled. It never would be settled until it would be decided whether slavery was to remain.[44]

Repeatedly Ward asserted that the United States must live up to the sentiments expressed in the Declaration of Independence. Or, as he said on more than one occasion: "The United States must return to the black man what was stolen from him--his liberty." He declared that the Founding Fathers recorded those marvelous principles on parchment-yet the frustration arose because America reneged on its promise.

He illustrated his common sense logic when he suggested that the Liberty Party return to their political grass roots. For example, after the election of 1849 he recommended that party members reactivate old-fashioned conventions. He said they needed to return to the very source of politicking. "We need to begin at the beginning of our cause and discuss our principles in their length and breadth." He asked the party members to go to the people and redefine the basic ideas of abolition. Success depended upon giving the masses the "truths we have to utter." These truths included the following:

> [S]preading our principles by building meetings, delivering lectures, holding debates, let us carry these principles to the firesides of our neighbors, to the blacksmith's shop to mill and to meeting. Let us organize in every town and country where there are Abolitionists enough to say one.[45]

System and method appear to have been bywords for Ward. He strove to convey the clarity and logic of his mind to others. That idea is borne out by Douglass, a contemporary of his who said:

> Mr. Ward especially attracted attention to that Convention. As an orator and thinker he was vastly superior, I thought, to any of us, and being perfectly black and of unmixed African descent, the splendors of his intellect went directly to the glory of race. In depth of thought, fluency of speech, readiness of wit, logical exactness, and general intelligence, Samuel R. Ward left no successor among the colored men amongst us.[46]

Moreover, one of his contemporaries wrote in *The New York Tribune* that Ward "was a man of ability, and as a public speaker has few superiors."[47]

As early as 1840 Ward's peers recognized his skill at debating. An antislavery newspaper noted that Ward had the "better of the argument" in a Liberty Party debate with Luther Myrick, editor of an abolitionist newspaper, *The Union Herald*. Here is an account from a witness at the debate: "But a good man and an able man, though brother Myrick be, he certainly fell into the hands of a strong man when he came in contact with Samuel R. Ward, with whom it will not do for every man to grapple, though young in years, consequently young as a disputant and but self-taught."[48]

More evidence of Ward's sound reasoning surfaced at an Abolition Convention in New York City in 1850. Two pro-slavery men--a Doctor Grant and a Captain Isaiah Rynders--attended the antislavery meeting with their rowdy friends who intended on breaking up the Convention and instigating a riot. There method included a sustained and constant heckling. At one point in the meeting Doctor Grant and Captain Rynders were asked to proceed to the speaker's stand and prove their assertion "that the Negro is not a human being." Professor Grant, according to *The New York Tribune* writer, "[C]ited naturalists, quoted Latin, talked of vertabraes, cerebellums, etc." He spoke of the African Americans distinguishing marks of inferiority, which he alleged excluded blacks from the genus *homo*. The Doctor claimed it a falsehood for the white man to call the black man his brother. Further he asked the audience to consider "the retreating forehead, the jet black complexion, the protruding heel, the wooly hair, its color, the thick skull, the long fingers, so like those of the ourangoutang and so unlike those of the caucasian man (sic)." As he went on the Doctor declared blacks to be a creature marked by nature to be a hewer of wood and drawer of water and nothing more. Doctor Grant claimed that by trying to elevate the black person the white person "disobeyed the law of nature and God's law."[49]

Incensed by the remarks audience member Frederick Douglass rose from his seat to rebut such gross distortions. In spite of continuous interruptions Douglass spoke to the issue. For example, as he enumerated the menial occupations to which black people were restricted someone in the audience hollered: "You would cut our throats if you could." To that Douglass replied: "Oh no, we would cut your hair."

A witness said Douglass "surpassed every speaker present,

including even the redoubtable Doctor, in the eloquence, pith and rhetorical grace of his address."[50] Then an annoyed Rynders shouted: "O, you are not a nigger!" You are half-blooded; a real nigger can't reason."

At that moment the Reverend Samuel R. Ward--a genuine Nigritian, black as the ace of spades in a deep cellar on a rainy midnight--took the floor, and fairly extinguished the party--learning, science, logic, wit, history--all went down in a heap, and the audience were (sic) thoroughly convinced that if anybody present was proved nephew of a rather dull ourang-outang, it was Professor Grant; if anybody was the first cousin of a very vicious monkey, it was Captain Isaiah Rynders. When their party evacuated the Tabernacle, they looked as if perfectly resigned to the discipline of crawling through a very small knot-hole.[51]

At first when Ward rose to speak he walked by Captain Rynders who yelled: "Well, this is the original nigger!" Ward retorted: "I've heard of the magnanimity of Captain Rynders, but the half has not been told me." He then proceeded to the rostrum and displayed his reasoning powers, finely-honed logic, and argumentative skill. Ward reproved the troublemakers as follows:

> This gentleman who denies our humanity, has examined us scientifically; but I know something of anatomy. I have kept school, and I have had pupils, from the jet-black up to the soft dissolving hues; and I have seen white boys with retreating foreheads and projecting jaws, and, as Dickens says in 'Nicholas Nickleby' of Smike, 'you might knock here all day,' tapping his forehead 'and find nobody home.'[52]

Witnesses at the event reported that the hecklers were overwhelmed beyond description. Biographer Frederick May Holland wrote: "Never was there a grander triumph of intelligence of mind over brute force. Two colored men (Douglass and Ward), whose claim to be considered was denied, had, by mere force of intellect, overwhelmed their malingers with confusion.[53]

The interrupted meeting became a well publicized event. *The Tribune* reported:

> But Mr. Ward was enough. His presence was the best confutation of the scientific absurdity which had been uttered. The intelligence, the command of language, the good humor and good sense, which he displayed, were irresistible. It was one of those instances wherein a simple

> practical fact falls and pulverises (sic) a huge pyramid of speculation. Never was the *argumentum ad hominem* used so triumphantly.[54]

To Ward, Black self-help emerged as the logical answer to the improvement of his people. He gave the concept a prominent place in his discourses:

> A depressed people cannot be elevated by any other than themselves. Others may remove burdens, plead their cause, afford them facilities, and cheer them with smiles and encouragement. But more than this they cannot do.

Ward argued that if all civil rights were given to black people and they did not respect themselves, abstain from alcohol, the gambling hall and the house of ill-fame, then they would deserve their condition. He continued with this line of argument:

> [I]f we wouldn't learn to read, and acquaint ourselves with the intelligence of the day; if we would not cultivate polished manners and refined sensibilities; if we would not fit ourselves for the society of the upright and the elevated; why, we should be just what we are; i.e., our present position would remain, morally, what it now is. In a word, self-elevation is the only possible elevation.[55]

Conversely if the black man did improve in the face of restriction he was an elevated person, "in spite of all the pro-slavery negro-hate this boasted, lying Republic is disgraced and degraded with."[56] Even a black man's bitterest enemy would respect him for his initiative.

Ward believed it logical to urge blacks to "Live above, not only the crimes and vices of the age, but above the mere fleshly and sordid of your nature."[57] Black people tending toward this way of life, had to "partake of the divine." As well, Ward instructed the white people to adopt new ways of treating black men and women.

> White man! Repent of your sins in head and heart and life, against the defenseless and unoffending. Elevate yourselves by rising above the petty demands of a devilish feeling, and stand up before the world as men whose fallen and depraved nature never can be fully restored, until you love your neighbor.[58]

Clearly Ward enjoyed a good debate. He knew that slavery contradicted God's law thus with that kind of backing from the Almighty he felt fortified with solid reasons when he had to argue against human bondage. Ward discovered that his ethical appeal and his emotional appeal did not win over audiences to his side as effectively as when he used his logical appeal.

Let us look at two of Ward's speeches that represent extreme examples of his public discourse. One is a speech to inspire young people to lead a Christ-like life. The other exemplifies Ward's rhetoric of resistance. The first example is an address that appeared in the second issue of the first volume of Ward's newspaper. Although it is impossible to determine if the printed speech entitled simply "Character" is the precise speech the Lyceum guests heard it can be assumed that since it occupied columns of The Citizen it is at least close to the one delivered. If Ward did rewrite the oration for posterity it doubtless contains the same general message.[59]

Ward wished for the young men that he spoke to in his audiences to immerse themselves in the doctrine of Christology. He would like to have seen more of them traveling and speaking out against slavery. He recognized that the young people had the stamina to prevail against the demanding regimen of the speaking tours. Thus, he had in his mind the idea of recruiting the young people when he spoke to the attendees of the Cortlandville Academy Lyceum on January 22, 1849.[60] Presumably the composition of the audience consisted of young men since remarks in the speech text reveal that he delivered the oration to young people.

That Ward had an established reputation constituted his appeal to the young men of the Lyceum. His ability to present a commendable speech went unquestioned. He impressed his listeners with his wide range of knowledge in the speech as he made specific reference to the Holy Scriptures, as he appeared secure in discussing ancient myths, and as he alluded to eminent authors and to historical figures as well.

Ward's ethical appeal is noted in the striking definition of his theory of Christology that he included in this speech. He said the central theme is unmistakably one which he wished for all men to believe: *The Ideal Character is Found in the Life of Jesus.* As we have discovered he formulated this theory through his education, his family's religious belief, and his associates in the movement. What is more, the encouraging and positive reaction he received from his auditors provided increased motivation for this task of discussing Character to these young men. Ward directed his appeal to the audience's sense of humanitarianism. He asked them to develop good character, give of themselves, and devote their lives to Christ's work.

Evidence of Ward's use of emotional appeal emerged when he

said: "Youth is, emphatically, the season of hope." And more, he appealed to the young men by challenging them: "For in youth, we lay the foundation of our weal or woe." He mentioned their need for discipline as he praised the determined character of Job: "Behold him when stripped of his vast possessions and when his pseudo-friends loaded him with reproach." Ward stirred the auditor's emotions when he spoke of the Lord's sacrifice:

> And shall I attempt to tell you how, amid reproach and scorn, and hate, and contumely subject to poverty, and all its long train of inconveniences, He bore himself aloft above the incidents of his condition, how he put his enemies to the pains and expense of exhausting their every malice in the invention of plots, plans and pretexts, for his destruction, and the overthrow of his system of atonement.[61]

He varied the emotional appeal by instructing his listeners to try and acquire an improved personality, develop better self-respect and, have a deeper reverence for Christ.

The life of Christ constituted the driving force behind Ward's logical appeal. He intended to tell his listeners that if they practiced Christianity they would become Christ-like. Essentially he told them:

> The very best I can do, is to hold up for your admiring gaze the man Jesus Christ, as the true standard of moral character and excellence. I do so, gentlemen, in full remembrance of the fact, that whether in realms of endless and indescribable bliss, we welcomed to seas of unalloyed, unfading, and increasing felicity, by the God Jesus Christ, depends upon our appreciation of our assimilation to the Man Jesus Christ.[62]

A benefit to which Ward continuously alluded concerned the personal satisfaction received through laboring in Christ's vineyard. He knew from personal experiences that "assimilation to the Man Jesus Christ" represented life's highest good. In brief, the epitome of character development is reached by engaging in the elevation of the oppressed. Cone expressed the same idea from another perspective:

> Jesus's work is essentially one of liberation. becoming a slave himself, he opens realities of human existence formerly closed to man (sic). Through an encounter with Jesus, man (sic) now knows the full meaning of God's action in history and man's (sic) place within it.[63]

Encounter with Jesus comprised the key to Ward's ideology. That notion was essentially what Ward conveyed to the students of the

Academy. The righteous character of Christ could not be doubted. Ward reminded his audience that other great persons of character had been sullied or guilty of misdeeds but Jesus Christ exemplified perfection. In this religious context Ward's logic worked most effectively.

Ward relied on definition as a rhetorical form in his discourse. He subdivided character into various elements such as integrity, decision, and simplicity. He defined those terms in the following way: He said Job, Daniel, and Jesus were examples of integrity. As to decision Ward declared: "He must take his (sic) election as to which course he shall pursue," that is, whether he or she will lead a life of sin or righteousness. As regards simplicity Ward remarked that, "this admirable trait is more fashionable among the more untutored sons of nature than in the halls of refinement." Two other elements of character he referred to were reason and conscience. The actual fact that Ward's reputation as an antislavery lecturer had been known in Cortlandville carried much weight with his audiences. His good will, intelligence, and integrity were not suspect. He would be expected to deliver a compelling as well as an instructive speech to the young students of the Academy Lyceum.

The second speech to be discussed is Ward's oration at Faneuil Hall, Boston on April 3, 1850. Ward joined with many other famous speakers on this day to protest vehemently the Fugitive Slave Bill. Again we encounter a situation of not knowing if the speech reported in the newspaper is the exact same one that the Faneuil Hall audience heard. But this example is as nearest to the truth as we can probably get.

Ward's qualifications to deliver the speech on the Fugitive Slave Bill were unquestionable. As a black man and a former slave he had been involved in the antislavery movement since his youth. Now, at age thirty he had behind him a wealth of experience and knowledge on the subject. Inasmuch as he had already expressed his anger at the bill the public anticipated a stirring oration. After all, he had written several editorials condemning the bill and he had delivered a raft of speeches criticizing severely the bill's premise. Over and over again he vowed to resist any legislation that provided for the recapture and delivery of runaways to their masters.

Some of the more notable abolitionists in the United States were present at this meeting in Faneuil Hall. In attendance were the vigorous Unitarian reformer Theodore Parker, a fugitive slave who ran away in 1848 disguised as a man, Ellen Craft, veteran of the Lyceum and antislavery speaking circuits Wendell Phillips, and the famous Boston editor and activist William Lloyd Garrison.

At the opening of his speech Ward established unity with his audience: "We have come here to make a common oath upon a common altar, that the bill shall never take effect." In this speech he moved the auditor's emotions with a much more energetic approach than the professionally dignified oration he presented at the Academy Lyceum a year earlier. This speech did not appeal to any religious spirit at all. It appealed to a spirit of resistance. He requested openly that his audience repudiate the Fugitive Slave Bill.

Reports of the speech reveal that the audience received it with a healthy response. Notations in the text say: "Applause," "Loud cheers," "Repeated rounds of applause," "Hear! Hear!" "Laughter," and "Loud Plaudits." Unlike the Lyceum speech this one seemed to have the speaker engaging in interplay with the auditors. Doubtless the energy exchanged between the speaker and the listener created a common bond.

In the speech Ward based his line of argument on the idea that higher law of Almighty God states: "Thou shalt not return to the master the servant that is escaped unto thee, but he shall dwell with them in thy gates, where it liketh him best." Those words were precisely what the audience wished to hear.

From the higher law of God Ward turned to making references to the hypocrisy manifest in a nationally known statesman's preachments. He asked what kind of influence can Daniel Webster have on admiring young lawyers when he favored the enactment of the Fugitive Slave Bill? That Webster and other civil servants decided on a person's destiny enraged Ward. He asked rhetorically: "This is the question, whether a man has a right to himself and his children, his hopes and his happiness, for this world and the world to come. That is a question, which according to this bill, may be decided by any backwoods postmaster in this State or any other." Again Ward displayed his ability to shape his oration to the occasion. He chose language appropriate to the situation in both speeches just discussed. And, he relied heavily on his instincts which had, in the past, successfully determined the nature of his audiences.

The foregoing speeches are not alike in their purpose and their proposition but they do serve as indicators of Ward's ability to speak to a wide range of topics. Ward had no difficulty in establishing his qualifications of intelligence, good will, and integrity to secure the approval of his audience. An intelligent individual with a logical mind his sincerity invariably received positive results. One speech portrayed Ward as a steward of the Lord while the other showed his aggressiveness in lashing out against the legislative arm of government. Logic emerged as the most significant element of Ward's invention which reflected also a deep understanding of the life of Christ. As Ward went forward with his mission to overcome oppression the development of his communication skills never regressed.

NOTES

1. Ward, (1970), p. 37.

2. Dorothy B. Porter, "The Organized Educational Activities of Negro Literary Societies, 1828-1846," *Journal of Negro Education* (1936): 557.

3. Porter, (1936), p. 575.

4. Ward, (1970), p. 53.

5 Porter, (1936), p. 575.

6. *The Impartial Citizen*, October 10, 1849.

7. *The Impartial Citizen*, November 21, 1849.

8. Ward, (1970), p. 40.

9. Invention is more than the planning and design of an oration, it is the utilization of all resources available to the speaker; it is the orator's knack of establishing credibility, the orator's ability to stir sympathy in his hearers, and his ability to develop effective proof for the case he is supporting. Caplan, (1954), p. 15. For further discussion of invention see the documents listed in the Speech criticism section of the enclosed bibliography.

10. *The Impartial Citizen*, February 20, 1850.

11. Ward, (1970), p. 114.

12. *The Toronto Examiner*, March 31, 1852.

13. *The Impartial Citizen*, November 9, 1850.

14. Ward, (1970), pp. 87-88.

15. Ward, (1970), p. 406.

16. Woodson, (1969), p. 195.

17 Ward, (1970), p. 63.

18. Ward, (1970), p. 277.

19. Ward, (1970), p. 291.

20. *The Impartial Citizen*, February 20, 1850.

21. Ward, (1970), p. 160.

22. *The Impartial Citizen*, September 5, 1849.

23. Ward, (1970), p. 42.

24. Ward, (1970), p. 255.

25. *The Impartial Citizen*, November 9, 1850.

26. *The Syracuse Reveille*, July 14, 1849.

27. *The North Star*, June 27, 1850.

28. *The North Star*, June 27, 1850.

29. *The North Star*, June 27, 1850.

30. *The Impartial Citizen*, March 14, 1849.

31. Ward, (1970), p. 43.
32. Ward, (1970), p. 43.
33. May, (1959), p. 351.
34. *The National Anti-Slavery Standard*, July 4, 1840.
35. *The Impartial Citizen*, October 5, 1850.
36. *The Toronto Examiner*, December 29, 1852.
37. Ward, (1970), p. 41.
38. Ward, (1970), p. 391.
39. *The Impartial Citizen*, April 24, 1850.
40. *The New York Tribune*, November 28, 1850.
41. *Syracuse Daily Standard*, July 3, 1851.
42. *The Impartial Citizen*, April 11, 1849.
43. *The New York Tribune*, May 12, 1847.
44. *The New York Tribune*, May 12, 1847.
45. *The Impartial Citizen*, November 7, 1849.
46. Frederick Douglass, *Life and Times of Frederick Douglass* (London: Collier-Macmillan, Ltd., 1962), p. 277.
47. *The New York Tribune*, March 10, 1857.
48. *The Colored American*, September 10, 1840.
49. *The New York Tribune*, May 8, 1850.
50. *The New York Tribune*, May 8, 1850.
51. *The New York Tribune*, May 8, 1850.
52. *The New York Tribune*, June 1, 1850.
53. Frederick May Holland, *Frederick Douglass, The Colored Orator* (New York: Funk and Wagnalls, 1891), pp. 183-185.
54. *The New York Tribune*, June 1, 1850.
55. *The Impartial Citizen*, March 14, 1849.
56. *The Impartial Citizen*, March 14, 1849.
57. *The Impartial Citizen*, April 11, 1849.
58. *The Impartial Citizen*, April 11, 1849.
59. See Appendix A and Appendix B
60. Lyceums were the commercial lecture platforms regarded as an agency for the spread of knowledge and the elevation of the intellectual and moral level of society. It is presumed that the Cortlandville Academy Lyceum was a part of a speaker's bureau attached to the Lyceum. For a discussion of Lyceums see: Robert T. Oliver, *History of Public Address* in America (Boston: Allyn & Bacon, Inc., 1965), pp. 459-466. See also Josiah Holbrook, *The American Lyceum: Town Meeting of the Mind* (New York: Oxford

University Press, 1956).

61. *The Impartial Citizen*, February 28, 1849.

62. *The Impartial Citizen*, February 28, 1849.

63. Cone, (1969), p. 35.

Chapter 7

Arrangement & Delivery

In this chapter I will analyze two canons of rhetoric-arrangement and delivery. That is, I will discuss Ward's arrangement of ideas (another term is disposition) and his delivery (referred to as manner of presentation) evidenced in his extant materials.[1] According to the available discourses it is apparent from the messages Ward prepared that he exerted a great deal of effort into organizing much documentation to prove his case in the body of his oral and written works. Ward considered the subject matter in the body of the discourse as the first imperative therefore the content had to be arranged methodically so that the speech topic became obvious to the listener. As to delivery Ward showed no signs of having any difficulty in the regulation of that canon. That is, he controlled easily his facial expression, his vocalization, and his body movement.

As I analyze the arrangement and delivery of the orations I will be using guidelines borrowed from classical rhetoricians as well as contemporary scholars. For example, the Roman orator Marcus Tullius Cicero's definition of arrangement is: "The ordering and distribution of the matter, making clear the place to which each thing is to be assigned."[2] Cicero said, also, that delivery consisted of "the graceful regulation of voice, countenance, and gesture."[3] The first canon I will consider is arrangement then I will analyze delivery.

Whether Ward's public discourses were in the form of a debate, a newspaper editorial, a Lyceum speech, or an oration at an antislavery meeting they were intended to inspire or to inform.[4] In his speeches to inform he educated his listeners about the unrighteous practices of pro-slavery advocates or informed them of the then-current occurrences in the abolition movement. His inspirational addresses were designed to motivate his auditors to renew confidence in themselves in order to reform their lives. But regardless of their subject matter his speeches suggest some effort to outline prior to their presentation.

The orations do, in fact, imply that Ward received comfort from one set pattern of organization. For example, editorials in *The Impartial Citizen* and other antislavery newspapers indicate a minimum of effort in preparation--he gave basically an account of his antislavery speaking circuit activities. Then, at other times he would discuss the condition of the African American people. If he included in his paper one of the speeches he delivered while on tour then he would exclude the lengthy introduction. In every one of his extant speeches there is a lengthy introduction, several supporting materials in the body, and a brief conclusion.

Unlike the editorials the introductions to the speeches were lengthy. These opening sections contained speaking forms that were characteristic of the Nineteenth Century. At the beginning the speaker expressed appreciation for the opportunity to speak, rendered a compliment to the previous speaker, showed a display of modesty, and made an apology in advance for any discomfort to the hearers. The following is an excerpt reported by a witness at a speech Ward delivered in Toronto:

> Mr. Ward remarked that it was his duty, according to the arrangement for the evening to give a somewhat statistical account of the labors of the Society (Canadian Anti-Slavery) through its humble Agent. This he knew would give him an opportunity even if he had the inclination to indulge in flights of oratory or figures of rhetoric. Besides, it was his misfortune to be obliged to follow one of England's noblest anti-slavery champions, John Scoble, Esq.; if ever, therefore, he felt like crawling into a very small space, this was the occasion. He (Mr. W.) proceeded to observe that he should give the statements demanded of him as briefly as practicable.[5]

On another occasion in an introduction he adhered to the traditional mode by conveying a modest estimation of his own importance: "To be on the platform with one of such positions, talents and erudition so distinguished and so justly beloved made me feel about as big as Tom Thumb."[6] Again, in a seconding speech he apologized with an apparant humility by remarking: "At this late hour of the meeting I did not expect to be called upon to address you and after what has been so well advanced by the reverend gentlemen on my right, I am at a loss what further to say."[7] But the situation did not diminish Ward's confidence as he continued to deliver a comprehensive speech.

In the body of Ward's speeches there exists no evidence of a particular pattern of organization other than his consideration to develop the main idea in as many different ways as he could invent. He related as much information as he could about slavery in many supporting materials. On the other hand, his editorials were usually about one problem. If the editorials did not address one problem then they were chronological accounts of his latest speaking tour. Occasionally he would cover two or three different problems but that seemed to occur in his speeches rather than in the columns of his paper. For example, in one discourse he included the following topics: the colonization of blacks, the American Church and slavery, Canada's admission policy for runaway slaves, and opportunities to farm land in Canada. In another instance, he covered many topics in a speech in Toronto in 1852. He discussed: Canadian people's attitude toward antislavery, *Uncle Tom's Cabin*, the Fugitive Slave Bill, the Canadian press, and the refugee settlement of Buxton. By covering so many topics Ward intended to give the audiences the full impact of slavery upon a society.

The supporting materials Ward utilized in his public discourses were: literary allusion, biblical parables, narration, examples, illustrations, statistics, rhetorical questions, a rhetoric of resistance, sarcasm and wit, the insult, and refutation. He did not include many varied rhetorical forms in his concise conclusions. In fact there does not seem to be much evidence that he pre-planned the end of his speeches. Seldom did he recapitulate the main ideas that were in the orations. Ward closed his speeches with fairly brief statements that were stimulating enough for the audience to ponder. Here follows one example of his conclusions:

> It is--Sir that the estimate that man put upon the Negro race will and does control their actions on the subject of slavery. And it is equally clear that the condition of the black people had much to do with encouraging or discouraging our cause. It is no less evident that such efforts do create and increase unfavorable views.[8]

Such an ending can induce ample speculation in a listener.

Ward included an abrupt conclusion in a letter to the editor of *The Colored American* in which he said that despite the fact that there were schools "open to blacks" examples of racial discrimination continued to exist in Canada. For example he reported that the Baptist Church at Brantford had the Negro pew system. Moreover, he reminded his readers that a black person could not become a Canadian citizen. However his sudden ending did include a strain of encouragement:

> I only beg leave to add, by way of conclusion, that the schools condemned by yourself and your "friend" are not exclusive; they are "open to all without regard to color," so is to be the manual labor school proposed to be established. Excuse my prolixity and want of system.[9]

Again I will examine speeches that represent the two types of communication used by Ward--the dignified and professional type and the resisting type. First I will consider the arrangement of the Cortlandville Academy Lyceum Speech. To begin, there is a central theme that emerges from the tightly organized oration. That theme is indeed in line with the belief of two contemporary rhetoricians Lester Thonssen and A. Craig Baird who state:

> It is assumed that the speech possesses a clearly defined and easily determined thesis or purpose; that this thesis is unencumbered by collateral theses which interfere with the clear perception of the principal one; and that the development is of such a character as to provide for the easy and unmistakable emergence of the thesis through the unfolding of the contents of the speech. That is to say, the critic is interested in finding out whether the speaker's conception of his task--be it to explain, to entertain, to convince, or to persuade--is clear, and whether the selection and arrangement of the ideas conduce to their effectiveness.[10]

In accordance with the requirement of those authors the arrangement of the Academy Lyceum speech does provide for "an unmistakable emergence of the thesis."

Of all Ward's extant orations this Cortlandville speech is the most effectively outlined and tightly organized. In the first few paragraphs he complimented the members of his youthful audience by noting they were experiencing their prime of life. He then went on to say they should capitalize on these precious moments, thanked them for the invitation to speak, and informed them that the title of his speech would be *Character*.

Following the introduction he stated the plan of his speech. He said: "My system is to discuss the elements of character, the importance of character, and the true standard of character." He adhered to the notion of favoring the distributive method of arranging his materials. That method is: "Having a common thought center and an obvious connection" among the different parts which are grouped in designated sections of the oration.[11] The speaker then spoke on the three perspectives of character as he intended.

The three elements of character were pieced together like building blocks in order to bring out the main theme. In one section of the speech he justified the description of the central thought by asking the audience to: "Study, I beseech you, this incarnation of perfection, gaze upon his *benevolence* until your bosom shall be filled with that which you admire. Behold his *humility* till you," pour contempt on all your Pride." The components of the internal arrangement of the speech directed their attention to helped to exfoliate the overriding point-of-view of character.

Ward dealt with the three components of character and then wished his audience success in their education. Finally, he hoped that they would be the recipients of "The acquirement and development of a Christ-like character." Thus, the arrangement of discussing character from three different perspectives aided in unfolding the central theme: *The ideal character is found in the life of Jesus*. The next speech to be analyzed will show a different approach in Ward's arrangement.

The speech on the Fugitive Slave Bill presented at Faneuil Hall in Boston on April 3, 1850 is the second speech to be examined. Although Ward followed the distributive method of arrangement in this oration it did not have the tightly systematic flow of the Cortlandiville Academy speech. (He appears to have indulged in some spontaneity). Ward began with an introductory statement of reminding the abolitionists why they had met on that day, complimented the speakers who preceded him, and then proceeded to undertake a blistering attack on the forgers of the fugitive slave law.

In the body of the address he rejected the law categorically. He did that by criticizing the initiator of the bill, a Senator Mason of Virginia. "That infamous bill of Mr. Mason, of Virginia proves itself to be like all other propositions presented by Southern men." He went on to attack the Northern dough-faces who allegedly compromised their position by approving of the bill. Then he rendered strong invective about Daniel Webster who approved of the bill. And, he shot hot blasts at the postmasters who were increasing their arrest records by apprehending runaways. Ward concluded with an intensely emotional-yet brief--statement that obviously punctuated his theme:

> And if our postmasters cannot maintain their Constitutional oaths, and cannot live without playing the pander to the slavehunter, they need not live at all. Such crises as these leave us to the right of revolution, and if need be, that right we will, at whatever costs, most sacredly maintain.[12]

Unlike the Cortlandville Academy speech the language of the Faneuil Hall speech tended toward the vernacular. It did not contain solemn notions about transforming lives as much as it had an immediate aim to condemn the evil legislation of the Fugitive Bill.

Of all the problems in the antislavery movement the fugitive law enraged Ward the most. It troubled him greatly that his country would allow men and women to arrest and enslave other men and women, especially when government documents proclaimed the very opposite. He asserted that he would resist any attempt at apprehension by protecting the runaways from recapture. A few months later he proved his statement of resistance by participating in the Jerry Rescue in Syracuse, New York.

In sum, Ward appears to have had one overall approach to the arrangement of his oral and written works. The majority of his messages were intended to inform or to inspire. Regularly he spoke out vehemently to reject or negate government policy.

Ward's introductions adhered to the traditional Nineteenth Century practice of taking the time to apologize before hand for occupying too much time, complimenting the previous speaker, and offering an expression of modesty.

The body of the speech manifested the crucial points. Extant materials reveal that Ward gave his undivided attention to the development of the main ideas within the body of the address. That preoccupation presumed to act on the main purpose of informing the audience of the evil inherent in slavery. Another purpose of Ward's public discourses involved the passing on of information to the activists in the movement. His conclusions in his editorials and speeches were for the most part, abrupt, that is, he did not bother to racapitulate or summarize what he said. The arrangement of Ward's public discourses however, show that the internal organization of his communications had a high priority in his speechmaking.

In addition, Ward accorded delivery a high priority in his speechmaking. An exuberant and vigorous speaker Ward delighted audiences with his enthusiasm and wit. An extremely impressive figure who stood over six feet tall, had a notably dark skin and weighed over two hundred pounds. He carried himself in a dignified manner, conveyed a strong sense of confidence, and all eyes focused on him when he spoke. Moreover, this imperious-looking orator always drew everyone's attention when he entered a room. His admirers said he spoke clearly and had a "well modulated tone of voice."[13] Wendell Phillips the Boston abolitionist and one of Ward's mentors said that he was so black that when he shut his eyes you could not see him.[14]

It is important to note Ward's ebullient manner of communicating a message helped him--in part--to become an effective orator. Strong physical action and a dynamic voice are not the only ingredients that captivated his listeners. He did discuss compelling subject matter. However the elements of delivery are important in the overall assessment. One excellent example of his delivery is found in a short speech concerned with the previously-mentioned runaway slave Jerry.

A close look at the recorded speech reveals eight exclamation points.[15] Those markings indicate an attempt to impose a high degree of emotion on the audience. Further study shows that Ward sustained the intense mood in the six-minute speech as he asked the audience a total of nine questions.[16] Employing his rhetorical know-how he queried: "They say he [Jerry] is a slave. What a term to apply to an American! How does this sound beneath the pole of liberty and the flag of freedom?" Again he shouted: "What value is there in our freedom while our hands are thus tied?" Witnesses said the hearers replied with deafening cries. Doubtless the success of this public speech pleased Ward. He sensed his ideas gained a special hold on audiences.

Needless to say Ward relished the excitement of the crowd. Here is a typical give-and-take session taken from a New York newspaper:

> But when we consider the case of men who are born on our own soil--who endure such crushings and oppressions as no people have ever endured--our people show a different feeling. Here I cannot agree with them. I am an American: (laughtercries of 'a black one!'). Yes, a black American! the

> son of a father who fought in the Revolution! (cheers)--a black citizen of New York--a black American am I--(applause)-gloriously black![17]

It is no mean task to imagine Ward exhibiting a notably animated delivery during that back-and-forth dialogue with the audience.

One element that affected Ward's delivery concerns the difficulty he had with his hearing. He told his readers in *The Citizen*: "We only hear in our left ear, the other has been deaf for thirteen years."[18] An impairment in his hearing may have caused him to speak louder than normal--as the hard of hearing are inclined to do. Understandably increased volume encourages a physically active speaker.

One of Ward's fellow abolitionists the Reverend Jermain W. Loguen who resided in Syracuse, New York wrote about his effective delivery: "[T]he impatient audience called long and loud for Samuel R. Ward, a distinguished black orator who made a most stirring speech, which was greatly applauded."[19] In addition Delany--mentioned above-- advanced a somewhat magnified description of Ward's abilities: "[D]ignity of manhood, without a superior in the crowded multitude, pealing forth in strains of majestic eloquence, bearing a living representation of those divine philosophers."[20]

It is unlikely that Ward delivered the Cortlandville Academy Lyceum in a physically vigorous manner. I doubt if he engaged in a give-and-take interplay with the particular audience on that occasion. The extant manuscript offers no evidence of intentional wit, humor, or sarcasm. The oration reflected a solemn and sober theme aimed to inspire young men to lead a Christian life. Any attempt to stir the emotions would have been in a pious rather than humorous vein. However, the presence of italics in the recorded speech indicate that a change in vocalization did occur. As we know italics are used to emphasize or to stress a point. Also, the use of many questions that address the direction of one's life can create a somber mood. For example, Ward queried: "But does he (sic) ever realize the objects of his (sic) highest hopes.? Does he (sic) ever make his (sic) deeds and title papers cover so many broad acres as to satisfy his cravings? Do his (sic) coffers ever contain enough of gold to still and hush his (sic) longings for more? No! No!!" More than likely when Ward mouthed these words he utilized a variety of vocalizations (a whisper, a hollow vibrating sound, or a booming voice) to underscore his feelings on the matter and to establish the gravity of the crime of greed.

Other markings in the text that imply a varied use of the voice are in evidence. Ward capitalized the phrase YOUNG MAN OF NAZARETH to obviously underline the importance of the theme. The phrase in capital letters leads us to imagine that this speaker who stood over six foot tall with a large physique and a booming voice could be heard easily in the Lyceum Hall.

It is esay to assume that Ward maintained a professional mood and a serious attitude in order to grip the emotions and intellect of the audience. The purpose aimed to inspire therefore the formal setting caused Ward to be less excitable with his gestures and his movements. Inasmuch as the subject of the oration concerned Ward's basic belief he steeped the message in religious allusions. Ward appealed to the listener's mental rather than physical faculties.

On the other hand, the public discourse Ward delivered at Faneuil Hall in Boston contained all the features of an intensely vigorous and physically active speech. He received numerous cheers and much encouragement from the auditors. That verbal feedback doubtless induced much more fiery delivery from Ward, that is, as the hearers respond they urge him to more intense speaking. It is not unlikely that the following excerpt moved Ward to active physical movement:

> Oh, this is a monstrous propostion; and I do thank God that if the Slave Power has such demands to make on us, that the proposition has come now--now, that the public mind is turned toward this subject (fugitive slave bill)--now that they are trying to find out the truth on the subject.

The type of word choice exhibited in "Oh, this is a monstrous proposition" has all the characteristics of inducing a lively delivery in the orator. Later on in the speech Ward said: "As I was saying, Sir," infers that Ward interacted on an intimate basis with the audience who then cheered for him to continue to castigate the slavocracy. Perhaps the one statement that brought about loud cheers is revealed in his vow: "I pledge you there is one, whose name is Sam Ward, who will never be taken alive.!" Then following that defiant outcry he referred to the right of revolution which indeed would cause, in most cases, a vigorous use of the gesture.

In general, Ward's appearance, his poise and self-confidence, his vigorous manner of speaking, his direct interaction with his audiences did much to capture the attention of his listeners and to create admiration for his ability as a speaker. His contemporaries admitted that the magnanimity of Ward's appearance, and his vocal and physical delivery influenced his hearers. From this assessment it can be ascertained that Ward received great pleasure by participating in the battle of wits with the public as he spoke out against the peculiar institution of slavery. Admired by his fellow abolitionists Ward endeavored to emulate the model man, Jesus.

NOTES

1. Nine of Ward's speeches are available to the researcher. Also, *The North Star*, *Frederick Douglass's Paper*, *The Colored American*, *The National Anti-Slavery Standard*, *The True American*, *The Voice of the Fugitive*, and *Provincial Freeman* contain contributions made by Ward. With the inclusion of the editorials in *The Impartial Citizen* the works total over one hundred pieces. In addition to Ward's autobiography there is an essay *Reflections Upon the Gordon Rebellion* (Jamaica, 1866) available from the University of Michigan, Department of Rare Books and Special Collections, Ann Arbor, Michigan, 48104.

2. Caplan, (1954), p. 7.

3. Caplan, (1954), p. 7.

4. Traditionally the purposes of speaking are classified into two types: the informative and the persuasive. Persuasive speaking includes three subordinates: to inspire, to activate, and to convince. (See Donald C. Bryant and Karl R. Wallace, *Fundamentals of Public Speaking* (New York: Appleton-Century-Crofts, 1969, Ch. 2). See also: John Wilson, Carroll C. Arnold, and Molly Meijer Wertheimer, 6th ed. *Public Speaking As A Liberal Art* (Boston: Allyn & Bacon, Inc., 1990, Ch. 6).

5. *The Toronto Examiner*, December 29, 1852.

6. *The Voice of the Fugitive*, December 17, 1851.

7. *The Daily Advertiser and Lawton's Commercial Gazette*, February 13, 1857 (Archives, Institute of Jamaica, Kingston, Jamaica.)

8. *The Toronto Examiner*, December 29, 1852.

9. *The Colored American*, March 13, 1841.

10. Lester Thonnsen and A. Craig Baird, *Speech Criticism* (New York: The Ronald Press Co., 1948), p. 393.

11. Thonnsen and Baird (1948), p. 394.

12. *The Liberator*, April 5, 1850.

13. *The Impartial Citizen*, April 17, 1850; *The Syracuse Standard*, August 19, 1850; and, *The New York Tribune* June 1, 1850.

14 Holland, (1891), p. 184.

15. The speech is recorded by Ward in his autobiography. Although Ward may have improved on the speech for reasons of posterity the mere description of the intensity attests to his feelings on the issue.

16. The seven hundred word speech probably took six minutes to deliver if Ward spoke at the normal rate of one hundred twenty-five words a minute.

17. *The New York Tribune*, May 10, 1850. There is no evidence to indicate Ward's father fought in the Revolution. It may have been an instance of what he referred to as engaging in "figures of rhetoric" or "flights of oratory."

18. *The Impartial Citizen*, January 2, 1850. He never explained how he lost his hearing. But the sometimes rough-and-tumble life he led may have occasioned an injury to the ear.

19. Jermain W. Loguen, *The Reverend Jermain W. Loguen As A Slave And As A Freeman: A Narrative of Real Life* (Reprint) (New York: Negro University Press, 1969).

20. *The North Star*, June 27, 1850.

Chapter 8

Style

The purpose of this chapter is to present an account of the Reverend Mister Samuel Ringgold Ward's style (the Latin term is *elocutio*) as revealed in his oral and written extant materials. According to the author of *Rhetorica Ad Herennium*: "Style is the adaptation of suitable words and sentences to the matter devised." Other definitions are: Jonathan Swift's "proper words in proper places," William Thrall and Addison Hibbard's: "The arrangement of words in a manner which at once best expresses the individuality of the author and the idea and intent in his (sic) mind." And, from the more contemporary source Edward P.J. Corbett: "All rhetorical considerations of style involved some discussion of choice of words usually under such heads as correctness, purity (for instance, the choice of native words rather than foreign words) simplicity, clearness, appropriateness, ornateness."[1]

Prior to discussing Ward's style it is necessary to describe the person Ward and the times in which he lived. In this way we will better understand the motivation behind the speaker's particular use of language. By the middle of the 1840's Ward had succeeded in establishing himself as a dedicated and highly respected worker in the antislavery struggle. In this well-deserved position, moreover, he carried himself in a confident and magisterial manner. That is, he assumed a dignified and distinguished carriage so characteristic among Nineteenth Century orator-leaders. This special attitude is discussed by Richard Weaver in his volume *The Ethics of Rhetoric*.[2]

In Weaver's discussion of the Nineteenth Century orator he reminds us that critics often dismiss the statesmen and stateswomen of the previous century as vain and egocentric. These same critics further complain that these men and women were so enamored with themselves that they were carried away with their own importance. Accordingly their lengthy public discourses which included innumerable biblical, literary, and mythical allusions allegedly bored their audiences.

Weaver argued however that perhaps these men and women were, in fact, magnificent personages. Or quite possibly they were equal to the importance afforded the hero of a classical tragedy. Weaver opined further that it may be possible that we are uncomfortable in the presence of such eminence and greatness because it implies that there were mighty men and women before us. In which case, the problem is ours and not theirs.[3]

It was the practice of these oratorical giants to predict their audience's behavior beforehand. By that is meant that in their time a "homogeneity of belief" prevailed among the people; the speaker knew the appeals cherished by their listeners. The people these speakers addressed held a high degree of respect for them. Therefore, the audiences elevated these men and women to such an eminent position in society that subsequently it set them apart from their neighbors. The aura of the "big man" (sic) which surrounded them conveyed the impression that they were speaking to "corporate humanity."[4] It is not uncommon among historians to propose that these great public speakers believed themselves to be Stewards of the Lord. In Ward's case, that is not a difficult notion to accept.

As to a description of the style of oratory of these speakers Weaver termed their extended passages of classical and literary references as "spaciousness." He described it as an opaque style, without qualification or specific reference. Although spaciousness came to represent a style of language immersed in generality the audiences received it with complete acceptance. Inasmuch as the orator's subject matter concerned matters of social responsibility; the age believed in progress; for these speakers to identify with humanitarian acts was not as unreasonable as it later appeared.

Ward's oration at the Cortlandville Academy Lyceum exemplifies the Nineteenth Century style of spaciousness labeled by Weaver. The style of this speech is significantly different from that of any other extant work of Ward's. As noted earlier the rhetoric is somber and serious without wit, humor, or sarcasm so prevalent in his other speeches. The piece contains an especially serious appeal. In the first place the discourse represents precisely what Weaver referred to as spaciousness. By the extensive use of religious terminology Ward spread before his auditors the subject of his speech "Character."

A traditional speaker Ward adhered to Cicero's statement that style is the adaptation of suitable words and sentences to the subject in question. Indicative of Ward's moral phraseology that he employed to keep in line with the religious theme are the following: "Buoyant with joyous recollection," "Sweeping along the moral heavens," "The homely garb of poverty," "A consciousness of rectitude," "The inspired volume ascribed to the Deity," "The fierce assaults of Satan," "Uzzean Job," "Israel's God," and "The testament in my hands."

The vocabulary used by Ward properly aligned with the message that inhered in the text. For example, certain words such as the following emphasized the proposition being delivered: integrity, decision, simplicity, reason, conscience, rectitude, self-respect, industry, and Christianity. Other words that reflected the greatness of Jesus Christ were: "Bright," "rare," "precious," and "cornerstone." Other references to Christ were: "Jesus, the Model Man," "He," "Him," "Christ," "Young Man of Nazareth," "Our Saviour," "Our example," "The Man Jesus Christ," and "The God man," Those words served as a constant reminder of the theme.

To keep up a steady reminder of the religious theme Ward garnished his speech generously with the names of biblical personages. In various passages the critic can find allusions to Job, Daniel, Abel, Joseph, Saul, and Timothy.

While the majority of this discourse on character is framed in a spaciousness style Ward did take a short rest and utilize an anecdote to illustrate a point: "The same fact, in another form, was noticed by a traveler, who happened to be present at an Indian council, the most eloquent member of which made, to the stranger's mind, a most thrilling speech, without receiving the least apparent attention, and resumed his seat unnoticed. In all their deliberations, not so much as an allusion was made to the oration of the gifted young chief. Astonished at the apparently unwarrantable neglect, the stranger asked the reason for it. He was told that a *falsehood* had once escaped those eloquent lips; he had thus lost his *character*, and with it his influence."[5]

Although the use of narration enhanced Ward's oration one drawback in his speaking style may have hampered the flow--the length of some of his sentences. Some of the sentences in the text are convoluted and peppered with commas. In a one-hundred and fourteen word paragraph Ward had three sentences.

> Behold it in the bright star of the Israelitish integrity, the young Daniel at the court of Nebuchadnezzar; Daniel, no place, power, threats, or what not, could serve from his principles, but who, in spite of all these, opened his windows toward Jerusalem, and poured forth his adoration to Israel's God. Nor could the starved lion, into whose dreadful den he was thrown, awe him into a dishonouring of himself as the price of the royal favor. His integrity he must maintain, and the God whom honoured thus, closed the voracious jaws of the terrible beast, and made him as harsh as a sucking lamb.

Such lengthy sentences appear to be awkward.

Even more unwieldy in the speech on Character is the following one-hundred and three word paragraph composed of one sentence!

> Nor am I at liberty to set up before you as the true model, upon which you are to form your character, that embodiment of moral virtues, Timothy, the youthful Bishop of Ephesus; nor indeed his patron and spiritual father, the young law student of Gamaliel, who when honors, wealth and fame glittered within his grasp, chose in obedience to his convictions of duty, to welcome a life of imprisonment, exposure, shame, suffering, neglect, reproach, and a death of martyrdom, instead thereof; like Moses, choosing rather to suffer affliction with the people of God, than to enjoy the pleasures of sin for a season.

If at the speech event Ward presented the foregoing two paragraphs smoothly then he illustrated his mastery of some cumbersome sentences.

In the Cortlandville oration Ward used a speaking style known as spaciousness. The language that inhered in spaciousness constituted an aura of religiosity which aimed to inspire young men of the Academy Lyceum to lead a Christian life. That central theme matched precisely the manner in which Ward conducted his life. Clearly, the underpinnings for Ward's behavior as a Christian Abolitionist were motivated by his definition of Jesus as the sacrificial lamb.

Ward's repertoire included more than an ornate and grand style of speaking. He revealed another form of speaking when he delivered the speech at Faneuil Hall condemning the Fugitive Slave Bill. His style in that speech reflected his direct and unembellished approach. The public discourse purposed to be volatile and vitriolic. He avoided a subtle approach and incorporated an unbridled language to inform the auditors: "We, the people, will never be human bipeds, to howl upon the track of the fugitive slave." Then, he criticized the law as a "bill which would attempt to make the whole North the slavecatchers of the South." No place in the extant text is there language that can be categorized as spaciousness. The word choice remains within the realm of the social activist.

The language of the social activist is obvious in the speech. Terms such as slaveholders, slavocrats, Northern dough-faces, slave-catchers, master, servant, fugitive slave, slave power, the right of revolution, and slave-hunter were used to adapt the speech to the mood of the audience. That the address is without elaboration attests to its impressiveness. From an analysis of the audience, the speech itself, and the occasion at Faneuil Hall Ward perceived how much had to be said on that day. He judged that by the mood of the crowd and the subject of the speech that he would keep the speech from rambling and go straight to the point.

To summarize the style of both speeches Ward followed in the tradition of a classical rhetorician and suited his language to the appropriateness of the occasion. He had the ability to present effectively a speech in a small village in upstate New York to an Academy of young men and then in an entirely different setting deliver a finely-honed diatribe against the fugitive slave law to a sympathetic audience in Boston's Faneuil Hall. One speech embodied the facets of a religious nature and the other waxed political. Through the careful use of language Ward capitalized on his skill and impressed his listeners with the full meaning of his message.

Other texts of Ward's speeches disclose the stylistic choices of the reformer. When he spoke to the crowd in Syracuse, New York about the runaway slave Jerry he used activist terms. He shouted: "A man in chains," "Not for life, but for liberty," "The curses of slavery," "The pole of liberty," and the "The flag of freedom." Aware that repetition can work on an audience he mentioned the terms "chains" and "freedom" at least ten times in that short six minute speech. Those evenly-balanced, contrasting words constituted an effective technique that hoped to stir the crowd to ask for more.[6]

A speaker who sustained his focus Ward's language of resistance evidenced itself in an article in *The Impartial Citizen.* Ward's deep concern for social reform is demonstrated in one newspaper editorial.

The title of the item--"The Despising of the Poor"--left no doubt in the mind of the reader that this discourse would be the product of a class-conscious activist. The catch-phrases he uttered in this speech were: "Toiling sons of want," "rich folks," "factory operatives," "Industrial classes," and "famine-stricken." He adverted to the rich exploiting the poor by mentioning how the rich "roil and riot in luxury." While he alluded to the ruling class as "wealthy neighbors" he referred to the poor as "famine-destroyed," "the dependent poor," and "poor neighbors." The language deliberately set forth Ward's reputation as a lover of the working class.

In the same discourse Ward's free-flowing style reveals also his understanding of how monopolies controlled the economy.

> Well; the poor mechanic and the laboring classes in almost every part of our country are becoming more and more depressed. Monopoly usurps the land, lowers wages, raises prices, contracts the circulation of money, holds all the offices, frames all the laws, and despising the poor, crushes him (sic) continually, and sets him (sic) at defiance. Monopoly demands that the poor shall pay high prices for manufactured goods, and buy in its market, and *no where else*. That the taxes shall, the most of them, be filched from the poor man's (sic) pocket, over his (sic) back and through his (sic) stomach; that the legislation or no legislation; and if any doubt as to the necessity of such legislation should arise, why, it gets up a war with some poor weak neighbor, robs him (sic) of his land and gold mines, kills off a thousand of our poor and his (sic) family and runs up such a debt as to make class legislation in the shape of tarrif taxation, a necessary evil![7]

In that section Ward poured forth a torrent of words remarkably descriptive of the exploitation practiced on the laboring class by the monopolies. The language in that piece discloses that Ward did not limit his protest to antislavery; he understood the economics of society and sympathized with all poor people.

In Ward's style of discourse he tried to advance his ideas by covering the topic from every angle to insure that his audience understood him. In a discussion about the annexation of Canada to the United States Ward took the opportunity to unleash a scathing attack on the "unprincipled American republic:"

> Many men (sic) look upon a future annexation of this beautiful virgin province to the blunted, besotted, rakish, unprincipled American republic. But let the antislavery discussion exhibit the facts in respect to that republic: despotism, its hypocrisy, its practical atheism, its abounding and ever-increasing snobbish aristocracy, its southern dictatorship and its northern servility, the utter recklessness of law, right, life, and liberty everywhere prevalent in the south, and the poor tame, cringing, crawling servility of the north.[8]

That abrasive language criticized the peculiar institution of slavery and showed evidence of a frustrated thirty-five year old activist. Not only did human bondage limit Ward's ability to function properly as a recognized citizen in America but the tentacles of slavery reached toward Canada. The words he selected contained information designed to discourage the possible annexation of Canada to the United States. He did not wish for the evil manifest in slavery in the United States to find its way to pristine Canada.

That penchant for listing showed up in other areas of his public discourses. For example, he instructed his people to continue to work honestly and arduously in their respective endeavors:

> I call the expert black cordwainer, blacksmith, or other mechanic or artisan, the teacher, the lawyer, the doctor, the farmer or the divine, and anti-slavery laborer; and in his (sic) vocation from day to day, with his hoe, hammer, pen, tongue or lancet, he is living down the base calumnies of his (sic) adversaries.[9]

More examples of his listing emerged when Ward offered advice to his people on how to conduct their lives, especially their voting behavior: "Preaching, prayer, hope, faith, men, angels, and God himself could not compel the enemies of such men to respect them."[10] The intention of listings is to impress or overwhelm the listener by piling on word after word.

Ward's petulance surfaced on one occasion when he revealed his annoyance at the disgraceful behavior of a black preacher in Toronto:

> Should you listen to his disgusting, abusive, indecent language and witness his semi-theatrical gestures, and you should see a large number of the coloured people of this city, if not a majority of them, you should join me in saying such things bedarken our prospects. Such is the state of things in Toronto.[11]

The petulance embodied a straightforward and unpretentious style that left no doubt in the audience's mind as to Ward's feelings on the subject.

Ward utilized the pun when he criticized Edwin Larwill the Tory politician in Canada who initiated a petition designed to create a more intense caste system. Of Larwill he said:

> In the first place, who got it--the petition--up, is by birth an Englishman, a tinner by trade, a noisy brawling, Tory politician. He has by some means tinkered himself into a respectable property which gives him some influence among the lowest class of whites.[12]

The all-inclusive "we" proved to be a useful term in Ward's public discourses. Some examples are: As ministers sometimes do, we must make a few concluding remarks." In an endorsement he stated: "We go with the Liberty Party." Subsequent to reading Thomas Dick, the Nineteenth Century philosopher-scientist Ward declared: "We believe in the future state as Thomas Dick."

Endeavoring to enhance his rhetoric with an aesthetic flair Ward concluded one of his works with a poem:

Lord when inequities abound
  And blasphemy grows bold,
When faith is hardly to be found,
  And love is waxing cold,
Is not thy chariot hastening on?
  Hast thou not given the sign
May we not trust and live upon
  A premise of divine.
Yes, saith the Lord, now will I arise,
  And make oppression flee
I will appear to their surprise
  And set my servant free.[13]

The stylistic device of the poem disclosed Ward's belief in a God that would ultimately intervene--that is, a God of deliverance.

Occasionally Ward relied on rhyme schemes to convey a thought. He tried continuously to persuade black people to move to the country. In that way they could be more self-reliant. He bristled at the beggars and paupers he saw in the cities. He remarked: "It would not be so, if everyone had land whereon to, raise his own ham, his chicken and his lamb, to shear his own fleece and wear it."[14]

In an effort to become more personal with his audience he used the conversational style in describing a convention he attended:

> We had singing, too, in the Convention.--And right good singing it was. Lucius Warner and the other members of the choir of Mr. Lee's church performed to the delight of all who heard them. That's no strange thing, for them. Now we do wish that singing was a part of all our liberty exercises. You can sing the evil spirit out of men and women when you can't talk it out of them. There is a kind that goeth not out but by fasting and prayer, and so there is a kind that goeth not out but by the charms of music. Had we any other music in us than that,
>
> "Which charms a savage
> Rends a rock and splits a cabbage,"
>
> We should get up some singing in our own hook,
> at every meeting we hold.[15]

Ward recognized that a more effective style of communication occurs when everyone is participating.

In addition to singing and poetry Ward had a fondness for the poetic couplet He commented on the pandering politician and opined: "When, therefore, Whigs and Democrats, in their State and local Conventions pass reformatory resolutions, although it is well known that they will,

> Resolve and re-solve--
> And then die the same.[16]

In other words, the promises offered by the party are never actually realized.

He mouthed more poetry when he wish to inspire his people: "As one of our own poets hath it:

> Honour and fame from no distinction rise:
> Act well your part--there all the honour lies."[17]

One line axioms conveyed his thoughts frequently. He noted that enslavement constituted: "That day that makes a man a slave takes half his worth away."[18] In another one line maxim he tried to recruit young people to do the work of the Lord: "Who will Feel the impulse and obey the call?"[19] He mentioned the slaves who could utter "words that breathed and thoughts that burned."[20]

Ward perceived the potential in language. He liked all of what it could do--that is, entertain, educate, inquire, assert, and pacify. Often he spoke in dialect. He joked about the Irish: "As some Irishmen say in a neighboring town: 'We go for *fradom*.[21] Once on a trip through Ireland he joked: "It's meself that's to blame for niver remimbering the gintleman's name at all, at all."[22]

The majority of Ward's colleagues acknowledged him as "a fluent speaker, an expert debater, and a good-natured fellow, full of fun and frolic. Barring his frequent references to his wife, his humorous sallies must always delight his audience."[23] Holland said Ward's speaking style impressed him as "intelligent, in command of language, a good humor, and enough good sense."[24]

Ward's extant materials indicate his fondness for words. He knew that if primed for the occasion he could without any effort venture into "flights of oratory" or "figures of rhetoric." His speaking style is placed into two distinct categories: 1) Straightforward, (the ancients called it the low or plain style) and, 2) An elaborate style (which classicists call high or adorned style) in which he used classical references, and literary allusions.[25] Within these two types of language usage he employed a variety of stylistic devices to communicate his idea of reform. His language embraced wit, sarcasm, stridency, and, at times impatience. To add variety he included the pun, the editorial "we," poetry, the rhymed couplet and one-line maxims appropriate to the occasion.

The language of the social reformer often emerged in his rhetoric, especially when he praised the humble poor and shot angry barbs at the vulgar rich. His word choice revealed his Christian Abolitionism when he praised the news of Jesus. Ward used words so effectively that his audiences were never at a loss from what he said. In sum, Ward's style communicated his Christology.

NOTES

1. Caplan, (1954), p. 7; Edward P.J. Corbett, *Classical Rhetoric for the Modern Student* (New York: Oxford University Press, 1965), p. 27.

2. Richard Weaver, *The Ethics of Rhetoric* (Chicago: Henry Regnery Co., 1965), Chapter VII.

3. Weaver, (1965), p. 166.

4. Weaver, (1965), p. 167.

5. *The Impartial Citizen*, February 28, 1849.

6. Ward, (1970), p. 87.

7. *The Impartial Citizen*, February 28, 1849.

8. *The Voice of the Fugitive*, February 26, 1852.

9. Ward, (1970), pp. 42-43.

10. *The North Star*, September 1, 1848.

11. *The Voice of the Fugitive*, October 21, 1852.

12. *The Voice of the Fugitive*, October 21, 1852.

13. *Frederick Douglass's Paper*, March 11, 1852.

14. *The Impartial Citizen*, March 20, 1850.

15. *The Impartial Citizen*, January 2, 1850.

16. *The Impartial Citizen*, October 31, 1849.

17. Ward, (1970), p. 95.

18. Ward, (1970), p. 224.

19. *The Impartial Citizen*, March 6, 1850.

20. Ward, (1970), p. 122.

21. *The Impartial Citizen*, February 28, 1849.

22. Ward, (1970), p. 249.

23. *The North Star*, January 25, 1850.

24. Holland, (1891), p. 184.

25. Corbett (1965), p. 27.

Chapter 9

Effectiveness as a Speaker

The foregoing rhetorical analysis has examined four of the five classical canons of rhetoric: invention, arrangement, delivery, and style of the Reverend Mister Samuel Ringgold Ward, a Christian Abolitionist. Ward's oral and written extant materials revealed three points: 1) that he had at his command a comprehensive knowledge of contemporary problems, 2) he utilized a reasonable amount of the rhetorical means available to the accomplished speaker, and, 3) continuously he demonstrated a positive effect on his audiences.

The critical examination of Ward's invention (ethical, logical, and emotional appeals) illustrated clearly a high incidence of logical reasoning as compared with the other appeals. Ward understood the benefits that could be derived from the careful use of emotional and ethical appeals but he relied much more on his ability to argue a case. His background and training caused him to trust in his own reasoning powers.

The arrangement of his public discourses suggest that he placed a high priority on the internal organization (the body) of a speech rather than devoting too much attention to the introduction or the conclusion. The introductions of the speeches appeared to be in the traditional mode unlike the introductions to the written works which were without the standard speaking form. His conclusions varied widely as he occasionally summarized but more often he simply closed out the speech with a brief statement.

Analysis of Ward's delivery revealed that he took great pleasure interacting with audiences. Moreover, he knew that the use of the body, the face, and the voice can be used effectively to appropriate special occasions. His large frame, his booming voice, and his lively presentation caused audiences to give their full attention to Ward as he spoke.

As to Ward's speaking style he would design his language according to the occasion. If he spoke to an antislavery meeting he would speak in the low or plain style. If he spoke at a formal occasion he would speak in the high or adorned style. Ward incorporated in his public discourses numerous rhetorical forms to develop the ideas in his orations. He would use the pun, the axiom, and the editorial "we." Other stylistic devices employed were: humor, sarcasm, invective, detailed description, and praise or blame. Without difficulty Ward adapted his ideas to his auditors needs. By the use of classical rhetoric Ward enabled himself to demonstrate his dedication to lead the life of a Christian Abolitionist.

One of Ward's contemporaries wrote of his oratorical effectiveness in *The New York Tribune* as "the ablest and most eloquent black man alive."[1] Loguen, mentioned earlier, praised Ward as a distinguished black orator who took his place among the great leaders of the day.[2] While on a speaking tour the abolitionist John Collins wrote to the upstate New York philanthropist-activist Gerrit Smith and reported: "Saml R. Ward one of God's noblemen is with us-he addressed the people of this city night before, last night--, and leaves this evening for Peterborough to attend a 1st of August celebration--His speaking was most excellent and effective--He is a splendid specimen of humanity.--"[3]

It is not easy to measure the success of Ward's stated purpose of bringing to the public mind, a clear understanding of the reform problems of the day. But his keen marketing ability increased the subscription of approximately five hundred for the unsuccessful *True American* to two thousand for *The Citizen*. Also, he enlarged the size of the paper from small quarto to full folio, and increased the frequency of its publication.[4] Moreover, other activist newspapers wished *The Citizen* success and ran items from it in their columns.

To understand Ward's effectiveness as an orator we need to retrace his activities as a reformer. We should be able to assess his impact if we recall the people with whom he shared notoriety as well as remember the beliefs he held regarding the need for deliverance of the people under oppression. An ordained minister he chose to become an antislavery laborer with the religiously-oriented abolitionists of New York State. This group had a reputation for being deeply committed social activists. Ward felt comfortable in their presence. Among the better-known reformers were H.B. Stanton, Joshua Leavitt, Lewis Tappan, Theodore S. Wright, and Henry Highland Garnet.

Those antislavery workers did not represent the William Lloyd Garrison wing of the movement. Ward did not share the speaker's platform with the Garrisonians since their religious orientations were notably different. It may have been that Ward knew:

> Garrison scorned the belief that the Bible was of divine inspiration; moreover, he was anti-Sabbatarian, holding that no day of the week was holier than any other and hence regarding as superstitious the setting aside of Sunday for religious worship.[5]

Rarely did Ward share the speaker's platform with Frederick Douglass. Both men had very different views regarding religion. Quarles clarified this point when he wrote:

> Douglass held such liberal views as to open him to charges of atheism. Partly due to his early association with Garrison, partly due to the inability of church groups to transcend color prejudice, and partly due to his disapproval of the poorly trained Negro clergymen (sic) who pandered to credulity and superstition, Douglass remained outside the field of organized religion. He was constantly contrasting the practices of churchgoers with their public avowals of brotherhood and love.[6]

Douglass and Ward agreed, of course, on the overall abolitionist cause but their methods to achieve their goals were different.

Since Ward labored with renowned activists in the movement and received numerous accolades for his achievements he proved himself to be an effective agent of humanitarian reform. As proof of his success he could select his audiences, the desired speaking occasions, and the geographic areas in which he worked. The public knew of his excellent speaking skills and requested his presence at antislavery meetings regularly. The historian Carter Woodson praised Ward as follows: "Coming to the aid of his race during the trying days of the abolition agitation, Ward took the platform and from 1840 to the passage of the Fugitive Slave Law of 1850 preached or lectured in every church, hall or schoolhouse in Western and Central New York."[7] An intelligent, effective, and dedicated Christian Abolitionist the Reverend Mister Samuel Ringgold Ward is rightly ranked by author-historian Gerald Sorin as on of the top ten abolitionists in New York State.[8]

NOTES

1. *Syracuse Daily Standard*, June 11, 1853.
2. Loguen, (1969).
3. GSMP, Syracuse University, Collins to Smith, July 25, 1851.
4. Edward Everett, Unitarian Minister, Statesman, and Orator is presumed to have subscribed to *The Impartial Citizen*. "Edward Everett" is scrawled above the banner on extant copies of the paper. In addition, other issues have the Harvard College Library stamp on the front page. Edward Everett served as a professor and as President of Harvard College.
5. Quarles, (1969), p. 43.
6. Quarles, (1968), p. 293.
7. Woodson, (1969), p. 193.
8. Sorin, (1971), p. 85.

Chapter 10

Findings of the Study

The Reverend Mister Samuel Ringgold Ward's beliefs and actions equaled those of dozens of African American men and women reformers of his era. Similar to those activists Ward held that the institution of slavery denied to a portion of mankind its birthright and endangered the civil liberties of all persons.

Ward's specific methods of resistance to oppression were through active membership in antislavery organizations as well as communicating his message by public discourse at the pulpit, at the speaker's platform, and in the press. Ward did not consider himself a militant willing to engage in hand-to-hand battle or open-warfare. But he did define "militant" as being combative in the struggle against oppression. Being combative consisted of communicating open resistance to tyranny through oratory, preaching, lecturing, and journalism.

In this approach to reform Ward intended to shatter three myths: 1) the myth of black intellectual inferiority, 2) the myth that all blacks engaged in anti-social behavior, and, 3) the myth that blacks were not serious about their personal spirituality. As he participated in reform activities Ward's dignified persona, his clergy status, and his command of language contradicted the message communicated by detractors who believed in the three myths that African Americans were dull, engaged in frenzied religious practices, and supported anti-social behavior. Ward believed the eradication of these racist notions would help relieve the suffering of the world.

Ward's personal campaign of proclaiming that all men and women regardless of their skin color could live together in mutual respect and love began in South Butler, New York in 1841. He believed sincerely that each group could educate the other out of their experience. When Ward worked as an antislavery activist in Canada he stressed "Scatteration," the wish for blacks to assimilate into Canadian society. Scatteration did not mean the erasing of any black consciousness as much as Ward meant it to show the black person from more than a provincial perspective.

Ward espoused the theory that a proper social and moral life will raise a class of people. Thus, he offered an inordinate amount of specific advice for black elevation. He endeavored to instill pride in his fellow blacks wishing for it to stimulate a will-to-improve. Conversely he devoted much of his public discourse to churchgoing slaveowners who were pillars of their church community and held men and women in bondage. To the slaveholders he said: "Remain in the church, but free your slaves." To politicians he said: "Change your attitudes within your party and take a stand against slavery." He believed that effective reform begins within the institution, that is, the peculiar institution of slavery.

As to Ward's thoughts pertaining to the United States Constitution he asserted many times that that document did not endorse slavery. The people were the ones in need of reform. But Ward's theory of Christology rose above all of the issues within the social and moral reform movement. Christology held precedent over other concerns. Ward's religious family background and his educational training were responsible for his having a deep appreciation for the miracle of Jesus Christ. Ward believed that similar to Christ he would bear witness and labor on the frontier of Christianity. He applied all of his efforts and knowledge to social and moral reform.

Ward employed his doctrine of Christology to illumine the misery among the oppressed--both in its personal as well as social dimensions. He tried to communicate hope to the individuals in bondage while simultaneously exposing the machinations of the ruling class. In a personal sense he revealed the contradiction between individual responsibility and the indifference to human bondage. In a social sense Ward did not attack the slavocracy or the organizations which supported the shameful slave system; rather, he offered solutions to the problem. Repeatedly he proclaimed that men and women must follow in the footsteps of Christ. Ward's moral imperative had its roots in his perception of Jesus Christ.

Appendix A

Speech on Character

An Address Delivered before the Cortlandville Academy Lyceum, on the evening of 22d January 1849, by S.R. Ward.

I deeply regret, Mr. Chairman, and gentlemen of the Lyceum that the humble response which I now attempt to make to your very kind invitation, must be somewhat meager in interest, owing to the extraordinary number of my private and professional engagements, for the last week. I have been obliged to speak ten times on as many different subjects, within a week, besides travelling (sic) some considerable distances. All of this, be sure would be but a sportive feat for a man of large capacity, but it is such a tax upon a very small modicum of power, as to make me feel much more like roiling than laboring. If you will excuse this poor, inefficient effort, and forget it, in consideration of my honest willingness to serve you, and in recollection of the better instructions to which you have listened from the gentlemen who have preceded me, and in anticipation of what you shall hereafter be entertained with, you may find patience enough to hear me.

Youth is, emphatically, the season of hope. Standing midway between childhood and maturity, it is buoyant with the recollection of the former, while unacquainted with the experience of the latter. The lights and shades, the joys and sorrows, which are interspersed amid the scenes; the thorns and flowers which are scattered along the pathway of manhood, are, to those in this interesting stage of life, like a *terra incognita*. And, as we are in our youth, unacquainted with what lies before us in the next stage of life, so we are too apt to pay but little attention to, what shall prepare us to act the part of men. All our prospects are painted upon the retina or our imagination's eye, in the greatest and most fascinating colors. We are our future selves, in the full enjoyment of all that is desirable, in human relations and positions. If letters is our chosen pursuit, we fancy that we shall not only enjoy, all the rights, immunities and privileges of *citizens* of the Republic, of letters, but we persuade ourselves that we shall be chosen Umpires in and over that Republic, waiting upon our vestments the insignia of its highest honors. If our attention be turned to the acquisition of wealth, we feel perfectly confident of success, and we suffer ourselves to entertain to other ideas than those connected with pomp and state, honors and obeisance as to the earning and homage of such a distinguished position as we shall occupy among ourselves.

Now, the steps by which we shall reach those towering ascents, the obstacles to be overcome, the rugged toils to which we shall be obliged to submit, the frowning face of Adversity which we shall have to encounter are matters not very intimately connected with, much less are they parts and parcels of the manhood, described in the poetry of our youth.

Yet an important, an immensely important, stage of our existence in youth--youth with its inexperience, its flowers, its fancies, its day-dreams, and its facility of giving to "Airy nothing A local habitation and a name with all its faults and follies *incalculably* important is this budding, blooming, hopeful season of youth.

For in youth, we lay the foundation of our future weal or woe. Not only the unreal and imaginary is entertained in the youthful mind; solid and substantial acquisitions are now and here made, which from their nature must be among the elements, if indeed they are not the chief elements of the future man, I mean not that youth is the season allotted to the acquirement of wealth, for, as a general thing, this is not true, nor do I refer simply to what is more important, the acquisitions of learning; but I speak of what is most important of all, the purposes to which youth is naturally devoted--the formation of Character.

As was intimated at an early day, I solicit your attention to this, as the subject for this evening's contemplation. My arrangement includes the following points, viz:

CHARACTER--ITS ELEMENTS--ITS IMPORTANCE, AND ITS TRUE STANDARD.

Of course I allude alone to good, correct, upright character. That which is worthy of the approval of the good, and which indeed, like

Pollock's Virtue, in the midst of hell, challenges the admiration of the most depraved.--That which maintains its virgin-like purity, when surrounded and offended by the vicious, as well as when associated with the chosen and the faithful of the earth. That which can afford to repose on its own consciousness of rectitude, whether it meets the smiles or frowns of the multitude, that which can feel itself supported alike, when arising to the surface of the social circle, or when depressed beneath it; brilliant alike in the rough and homely garb of poverty, so arrayed in the "purple and fine linen" of some modern Dives.

Character, so defined and described, may be said to be but a rare plant among us. This point I do not purpose to discuss. Sufficient is its forms now to repeat that the beautiful and interesting season of life which is yours, gentlemen of the Lyceum, is the season when more is done to form, acquire, and develope (sic) character, than at any other; and that what is now done, and well done, will leave [word garbled] traces upon your future selves not only, but lay broad and deep the basis of your happiness in this life, and that beyond the grave. At the same time, if from thoughtlessness or whatever cause, this stage of your experience be so neglected or perverted, as that an unhappy inclination be given you now, lasting in time, and ceaseless beyond time, must be the fruits--the bitter fruits thereof.

What are among the most essential elements of upright character?

In a most conspicuous position among them stands--indeed, at the very basis of them lies--that bright, rare, precious, corner-stone, *integrity*, a happier (word garbled) which never adorned the character of an Angel. It is on almost every page of the inspired volume ascribed to the Deity as the grand and glorious testing ground of the Christian's faith. It is a trait, too, as indispensable as it is brilliant, in the character of any earthly or celestial intelligence. It is that unswerving, immovable, appreciation and choice of the right, which causes the *wrong* to be seen, in all its hideous monstrosity; which makes it impossible for vice to array herself in a garb so attractive, to utter words so suasive, in sounds so musical as to captivate and seduce. If this be regarded as saying too much, sure I am that even profane history furnishes most admirable examples of it. It was this incorruptible trait, which has made the moral firmness in the character of a Roman proverbial down to this day.

But witness it in the character of "Uzzean Job." Behold him when stripped of his vast possessions, bereft of his children, and subjected to the evil councils of the wife of his bosom, while about his hearth-stone were friends--pseudo-friends--who in their infatuation of misanthropy, or both, loaded him with reproaches unswerved by the astounding suddenness of his reverses, undismayed at the

"selfish council of those hangers-on,"

"unshaken" in the near face to face view, into which he had been thrown with stern visaged *Adversity*--unseduced by the appeal made to his impatient impulses by his wife, and unterrified by the fierce assaults of Satan, like a bold rock in the mid-ocean which defies the surge, yields not to the wave and says aha! to the billow--he stands erect and looking his God in the face, exclaims--"Until I die mine *integrity* shall not depart from me!"

Behold it in that bright star of Israelitish integrity, the young Daniel at the court of Nebuchudnezzar; Daniel, whom no place, power, threats, or what not, could swerve from his principles, but who, in spite of all these, opened his windows toward Jerusalem, and poured forth his adoration to Israel's God. Nor could the starved lion into whose dreadful den he was thrown, awe him into a dishonoring of himself as the price of the royal favor. His *integrity* he must maintain, and his integrity he did maintain, and the God whom he honored thus, closed the voracious jaws of the terrible beast, and made him as harmless as a sucking lamb.

I might mention that splendid constellation of young men, whose names and deeds are furnished to our hands by the inspired writers, beginning with Abel, pausing to admire Joseph, paying a merited tribute to the three Hebrew children, and so sweeping along the moral heavens, we might take in the range of our view Saul and Timothy, and a host of others, of equal glory and brilliancy.

But above them all the great central Sun of our moral system, shines in infinite splendor and effulgence, *Jesus, the Model Man.* And shall I attempt to tell you amid reproach and scorn, and hate and contumely subject to poverty, and all its long-train of inconveniences, privations and exposures, He bore himself aloft above the incidents of his condition, how He put His enemies to the pains and expense of exhausting their every malice in the invention of plots, plans and pretexts, for his destruction, and the overthrow of His system of atonement! No, gentlemen, I will content myself with pointing you to the simple, and ample story of his life, and character, and death, as written by his immediate friends and followers. There shall you learn what is more valuable, more reliable, more exemplary, in respect to integrity of character, than is to be found in all the biographies of all the men of whom pens have ever written.

Another, and an analogous element of good character, is Decision. No appreciation of the virtuous and commendable, however high to practice, if it be not stable. A man needs not only to choose goodness, for his own sake, but he needs the moral nerve, to abide his choice in the storm as well as in the sunshine, under frowns and reproaches, as well as when met by courteous homage. Not unfrequently, in these times, are we called upon to embrace truths emanating from God's own heart, of whose origin and character, we have no more doubt than we have of the being of Jehovah, of the authenticity of his word. And yet the very recognition of the divine authority, which we find in such truths, will expose us to circumstances anything else than pleasant and desirable. Now the acknowledgment and embracement of truth is one of the lowest conditions upon which we can maintain our integrity. Nay, more, the avowal and the defense of truth is not unfrequently altogether vital to one's maintenance of integrity; and if integrity be wanting, good character cannot exist. When one is placed where he must conceal, disavow, or deny his principles, (which is but another name for denying his God,) or lose the favor of some powerful benefactor, and incur the reproaches of those whose opinions are generally esteemed, he must make his election as to which course he shall pursue. If he lacks the decision to tread the path in which, according to his convictions, truth leads, as she smiles and beckons him onward, then there is that deficiency in his character which is nothing less than a destitution of one of its key-stones and corner-stones.--A Joseph, a Daniel, he never can be, and what is worse, a follower of Jesus he can scarcely be, for the *cross bearing element* his character does not contain;--And any transforming or regenerating process through which he thinks he has passed has done but very little good, if it has not supplied this deficiency. A practically, and a reliably good character, *without decision*, is a moral phenomenon which is yet to be witnessed.

Prominent among the sparkling traits of all the men whose names have come down to us on the historic page, who were great on account of their goodness, is Simplicity. To the shame of our civilization be it spoken, we find this admirable trait more frequent among the untutored sons of nature than in the halls of refinement.

Where nature unadorned, and unsophisticated, he left unspoiled by this and that form of fashionable duplicity; there we see this important element of character in its native power and brilliancy. Society is too frequent a refinement of deceit; its sentiments a bundle of prejudices; its commerce a set of measures for reciprocal deception and overreaching simplicity, straight forwardness, open handed honesty, therefore, in not so much a matter of fashion among us as it ought to be. Yet the very rareness with which it is to be found, makes it the more precious. That a man cannot trade without being constantly exposed to the varied forms of penny-wise knavery is indeed deplorable. But that he should suffer himself to become fraudulent and deceptive, like too many of his neighbors, is still more deplorable. That a man should find so little of the reliable in the coined expression, and honed professions of his neighbors is grievous indeed. But that he should become one in heart, and practice, with them, is much more grievous. In truth, the more subtle, the more ambiguous, the more deceptive, is the state of society around us, the more *simplicity* of character do we need to counter act who overcomes it. If we allow men (sic) in this particular, to impress upon us their own image we are "overcome of evil" instead of "overcoming evil with good."

If, gentlemen, being environed as you are, by as many forms and names of an opposite sect, by fixing your gaze upon too high and holy examples set before you in the Scripture and by making them the models upon which you determine to form your characters, you [line blurred] your impression upon the age in which you shall live, shall be both healthful and imperishable.

God has ordained--most wisely ordained--that character, to be good must be under the containment of reason and conscience, and that they both shall bow in meek and complacent subjection to the moral law. That law not only comes to us under the most sacred sanctions, as an emanation from the Supreme legislative power of the Universe, but it comes in perfect adaptation to our circumstances in general, and especially to that important stage of our life which is peculiarly allotted to the formation of character.

It unfolds to us the matter and degree of control we should exercise over the passions and appetites; the light in which we should regard our Creator; and the sacredness in which we are to hold the rights and the interests of our fellow men (sic). It sets up before us a perfect standard, a perfect model, and a perfect set of rules, in accordance with which, it lays us under the most solemn obligation to form our character and direct our life. It then, is the benignity which originated itself, warns us on the one hand to shun the disastrous consequences of heedlessness or disobedience to its mandates, and on the other hand promises the most desirable results from a close, and rigid, and life-long adherence to its reasonable, profitable, and merciful requirements. To indulge the dreamy phantasy, for one single moment, that he who has erected for us such a standard, and proffered us such aid, and given us this highest and best of all models, should not suffer us to flounder and grope in our weakness and blindness forever; unable to arrive at that which we seek, if we neglect His law, is to rush into the wilds of disappointment, and to drink the bitter dregs of the most wretched experience.

But if reason is suffered to maintain the control of passion, and conscience shall sit always as reason's umpire, and the divine law shall rule supreme over all, we shall, in spite of evil examples without, and evil tendencies within, be enabled to form and to secure that greatest of all blessings in this world and that to come--a good character.

II. My second point is the importance of character. I shall make but a very small draft upon your patience in the discussion of this and the remaining portions of the subject: an (sic) thinks himself wisely employed, and his followers in the main give him credit for wisdom, when he devotes his early risings, his late retirings, his sweaty toil, or his brain's most laborious exercise, to the gathering up of wealth. If success crown his efforts, after many years of alteration of hope and fear, the wisdom of his devotion to his favorite good but few will venture to question. But does he ever realize the objects of his highest hopes? Does he ever make his deeds and title papers cover so many broad acres as to satisfy his cravings? Do his coffers ever contain enough of gold to still and hush his longings for more? Has he when most successful found that amount of this world's goods which fills up the desires of an immortal spirit? In fine, has he acquired a *permanent possession*? No! No! His riches may take wings and fly away. The curling crackling flame, the mighty tempest, the flood, the wave, may the next moment dash to earth the tenure by which he holds his boasted goods. *Not so with character.*

The man (sic) makes a good disposition of his time and his powers, who devotes both to the obtainment of learning. He may say with Bacon "Knowledge is power," and by honest industry and patient mental toil, he may become among the most powerful of earth's favorite sons. But if with this "getting," as the wise man hath it, he gets not understanding. "the fear of the Lord which is the beginning of wisdom," another name for a [line missing] be abused and perverted, and made to him and his fellow men (sic) a *curse* instead of a *blessing*? Who knows but that his power, like Alexander's and Napoleon's, may be applied to evil rather than good? What safeguard is there that his wit and skill will not be devoted to the devising of schemes for the supplanting of his (sic) fellow; the oppression of his brother?--The only security we can have against these consequences is,-not the laws, not the mere restraints of civilization, as they are called, but the character, the upright character of the man possessing this power. When his character is a scintillation of God's, his *power* may be; and then it will be safe. Then he will have acquired a permanent possession not only, but a possession, the more he (sic) acquires of which, the better it is for his neighbor, his poor dependent, helpless and defenceless (sic) neighbor. Can so much be said of wealth, or mere learning?

Riches and knowledge, when estimated according to their real value, and devoted to their appropriate uses, are no mean possessions. But when the happiest facilities are afforded for their obtainment some of us can neither be learned nor rich. I am myself among the number. But the poor man--the poorest of men (sic)--whose character is unimpeachable, whose good name is untarnished, has a *passport to human favor* which more than supplies the lack of other good.

"The honest man tho' e'er so poor,
Is king of men for a' that."

In countries where poverty passes from generation to generation, by a sort of entail, or where certain *external peculiarities* mark out some men, as according to certain *high authority*. "doomed men," or "doomed races," not unfrequently do you see some of these very same "doomed men," through the force of their uprightness and energy of character, arise superior to the influences which crush them, and extort from those who "doomed" them, the well earned credit of an upright character.

Politicians have addled their brains, at one time and another, to produce, and to prevent to their fellow citizens, such a system of legislation as should most, or best, conduce to what is called a "credit system." When I became 21, this was one of the most exciting, difficult, and strife engendering of all the family of political *questiones vexiate*. But the plain truth is, legislation is as impotent as the infant of yesterday, to make a basis or system of credit. That matter lies altogether in another direction. *The only real and true basis of* CREDIT is CHARACTER. Wealth is but *ability* to pay an honest demand. Law may force the unwillingly able to pay what he would not, otherwise. But neither wealth nor law gives a man credit. A man's credit depends, among men of sense, among men of real discernment, upon the character he (sic) possesses, whether rich or poor. When you trust wealth, or trust law, you trust not man (sic). But when you trust a man (sic) for what he is, for what his character is, you trust him (sic). *This basis of true credit*, whatever may be done by, or whatever may become of legislation, is character.

The importance of character is seen in the fact, that it is indispensable to internal harmony, or self-respect. In vain does the voice of partial friends, on this hand and on that, flatter me with soft encomiums, in vain does the wife of my bosom express to me, in terms and tones the tenderest affection, her hearty and cordial approval of my character; in vain do my children hold me as the standard of moral excellence;--if all the while I know that the state of my heart is the subject of the constant clamoring of my conscience--that betwixt these two elements of my moral nature, there jarring is discord--that while all others respect me, I cannot respect myself. But when the music of internal harmony is to be [blurred words], when from consciousness of [blurred sentence] reproached by my nearest, dearest friends as well.

We have seen in a meeting of Quakers, the words of one man, a small man, a poor man he might be, a young man, (sometimes a woman) outweigh the words of a whole meeting, in one of their religious discussions. Now, that person, so far from being the most eloquent member of the body, is often the least gifted as an orator. But still, his voice controls.--To him all pay deference; and the grave members feel no doubt, that their decision receives the sanction of the Great Head of the Church. Now, what is the secret of this man's power? The coolness and strength of his judgment, has much to do with it, be sure, but that is only an element of the controlling (sic) attributes: it is the influence of his UPRIGHT CHARACTER.

The same fact, in another form, was noticed by a traveller (sic), who happened to be present at an Indian council, the most eloquent member of which made, to the stranger's mind, a most thrilling speech, without receiving the least apparent attention, and resumed his seat unnoticed. In all their deliberations, not so much as an allusion was made to the oration of the gifted, young chief. Astonished at this apparently unwarranted neglect, the stranger asked the reason of it. He was told that a *falsehood* had once escaped those eloquent lips; he had thus lost his *character*, and with it his influence.

Quakers and Indians are not the only men (sic) among whom one's influence depends upon his character. Poverty, ignorance, nothing can, in the long run, deprive the man of probity of character of that influence which belongs to moral worth. CHARACTER is the best ground, the only true ground of MORAL INFLUENCE.

But gentlemen, there is one more method of estimating the value of character, to which I will now ask your attention. It is a view of what *God does to promote it*, and a consideration of the *rewards* which He confers upon it. That we may form a correct character, he placed before us the best possible model, the highest possible standard, and the most moving inducement, and the happiest facilities, the model He gave us is Himself, the standard is His Word, as contained in the Law and the Gospel. The inducements, are the internal satisfaction arising from doing right, and the good influences we may exert upon or fellow men (sic); and the rewards of an everlasting life, in which is to be enjoyed the completest, most perfect felicity. The facilities referred to, are the aids and encouragements He, in infinite grace, bestows upon us, to enlighten and cheer us in the rugged labors to which we are called, not the least of which is the overcoming of the obstacles *within ourselves* which is in the way of forming a good character.

It is not possible too frequently or too strongly to urge upon your attention, the fact, that character to be *correct* must be Christian; while the Christianity which does not embody integrity, decision, and a complete, invariable, universal subjection to the Divine Law of Rectitude, is without a Bible warrant, destitute of a likeness to Christ, unfit for life, and unsafe for death. The rewards, therefore, which God holds out to the hope of the Christian, are but rewards for the formation and maintenance of good, upright, and Christian character. Such is God's estimate of it.

My method includes as its third particular, the

True Standard of Character

To this allusion has been made. And now, to speak at the same time with brevity and fullness, let me say, THAT STANDARD is the young man--the poor YOUNG MAN OF NAZARETH. You did not call me here to preach you a sermon, gentlemen, but it is well enough that I should say that I have here, as elsewhere [sentence missing] our Saviour--as Man, He is our example--While I recollect that I am not here to preach, I take it that I am here to do the best I can with the subject before me. The very best I can do, is to hold up for your admiring gaze the Man Jesus Christ, as the true standard of moral character and excellence. I do so, gentlemen, in full remembrance of the fact, that whether in realms of endless and indescribable bliss, we shall be welcomed to seas of unalloyed, unfading, and increasing felicity, by the God Jesus Christ; depends upon our appreciation, of our assimilation, to the Man Jesus Christ.

I do not present to you, therefore, as the true standard of character, Joseph, who, according to the Mosaic record, was assailed by one of the most seductive temptations ever presented to a young man, presented too, I doubt not, by a beautiful fascinating woman (certainly she was according to my standard, for she was an Egyptian, a black woman) but who met this temptation, in the unwavering rectitude of his integrity, and welcomed a felon's cell rather than a felonious character. Nor do I dare to lace before you as the standard of character, that bright galaxy of young men to whom reference was made in a former part of this discourse, whose integrity of character enabled them most triumphantly.

"To weary tortures and rejoice in fire;"

whose trueness of heart made them; in the very furnace blaze, chosen associated for the "form of the fourth, which was like the Son of God."

Nor am I at liberty to set up before you as the true model, upon which you are to form your character, that embodiment of moral virtues, Timothy, the youthful Bishop of Ephesus; nor indeed his patron and spiritual father, the young law student of Gamaliel, who when honors, wealth, and fame glittered within his grasp, chose in obedience to his convictions of duty, to welcome a life of imprisonment, exposure, shame, suffering, neglect, reproach, and a death of martyrdom, instead thereof; like Moses, "choosing rather to suffer affliction with the people of God, than to enjoy the pleasures of sin for a season." No, gentlemen, luminous as are all these examples, encouraging as they are to us, as they present before us in the aspect of indubitable, unquestionable history, to what practicable heights of holy attainments human character has risen by the divine aid; weighty as is the condemnation under which they lay us, if we make not like attainments, brilliant as they are, as both specimens and demonstrations of what human nature is capable when God's sublimating influences and energies are applied to it, yet still would I not dare, with the Testament in my hands, with the Gospel in that Testament, present even one of these, as the pole star to guide your bark safely amid the rocks and quick-sands, which on every hand beset your course across the ocean of life, as the sun around which you are to revolve, and whence you are to derive that light and heat which shall illumine, cheer and warm you into present, future, and eternal life.

But, gentlemen, reminding you once more, that above wealth, learning, and all other real--not to speak of fancied good--you and i and all of us depend, while on earth, and when done with earth, upon our character; and alluding once more to the unspeakable importance of this greatest of all acquisitions, let me point you to that sacred, incomparably perfect and holy standard of rectitude, the God Man. Study, I beseech you, this incarnation of perfection, gaze upon His benevolence until your bosoms shall be filled with that which you admire. Behold His humility till you

"Pour contempt on all your pride."

Follow Him, from His manger-cradle to His [word blurred] cross, till His image shall be impressed [sentence missing] of the Lyceum; allow me to wish you the most abundant success in the noble and mind magnifying objects which engage your attention, and occupy your time, in this, your collective capacity. And may God grant, that in intimate connexion (sic)--indeed, a very apposite connexion (sic)-with your literary pursuits, you may be blessed with that wisdom, that humility, which shall induce you practically to appreciate, the great and glorious end of books, letters, law, time, education,--life itself.

THE ACQUIREMENT AND DEVELOPMENT OF A CHRIST-LIKE CHARACTER

OUTLINE OF SPEECH ON CHARACTER

An address delivered before the Cortlandville Academy Lyceum on the evening of the twenty-second of January, 1849 by Samuel R. Ward.

INTRODUCTION

Statement referring to activities of past week. Traveled considerable distance. That is a tax on my constitution. Excuse this poor effort.

Statement referring to the audience. Youth is the season of hope and recommendation to prepare for manhood.

CENTRAL IDEA STATEMENT: The ideal character is found in the life of Jesus Christ.

Transitional statement: My arrangement for this speech is:

Character - Its Elements - Its Importance - and Its True Standard.

I. Essential Elements of Character.

A. Integrity

1. Examples are on every page of the Scriptures.
(1) in the character of Job
(2) behold it in Daniel
(3) in a constellation of young men

a. Abel

b. Joseph
c. Saul
d. Timothy

B. Decision.

1. Men and women need moral nerve to make the right choices.
2. Frequently we must choose between God's word and the word of others.
3. We must select the right course to pursue.
4. Reliably good character does not exist without the element of decision.
C. Simplicity.

1. Found in the untutored sons of nature rather than in the halls of refinement.
2. Its rareness makes it more precious.
3. We need less deceit and more simplicity of character.

II. The Importance of Character

1. The young man of Nazareth is an example.

(1) Jesus is the true standard of moral character and excellence.
(2) Not Joseph or Timothy, but the rectitude of the God-Man.

CONCLUSION

2. Allow me to wish you success.

(1) May God bless you with wisdom and humility
(2) May you realize the end of life itself is
THE ACQUIREMENT AND DEVELOPMENT OF A CHRIST-LIKE CHARACTER

Appendix B

Speech on the Fugitive Slave Bill

An address delivered at Faneuil Hall, Boston, Massachusetts on April 3, 1850 by Samuel R. Ward.

I am here tonight simply as a guest. You have met here to speak of the sentiments of a Senator of your state whose remarks you have the honor to repudiate. In the course of the remarks in the gentleman who preceded me, he has done us the favor to make honorable mention of a Senator of my own State--Wm. H. Seward. (Three hearty cheers were given for Senator Seward).

I thank you for this manifestation of approbation of a man who has always stood head and shoulders above his party, and who had never receded from his position on the question of slavery. It was my happiness to receive a letter from him a few days since, in which he said he would never swerve from his position as the friend of freedom. (Applause).

To be sure, I agree not with Senator Seward in politics, but when an individual stands up for the rights of man against slaveholders, I care not for party distinctions. He is my brother. (Loud cheers).

We have here much of common cause and interest in this matter. That infamous bill of Mr. Mason, of Virginia, proves itself to be like all other propositions presented by Southern men. It finds just enough of Northern dough-faces who are willing to pledge themselves, if you will pardon the uncouth language of a backwoodsman, to lick up the spittle of the slavocrats, and swear it is delicious. (Applause).

You of the old Bay State--a State to which many of us are accustomed to look as to our fatherland, just as well look back to England as our mother country--you have a Daniel who has deserted the cause of freedom. We, too, in New York, have a "Daniel who has come to judgment," only he don't come quite fast enough to the right kind of judgment. (Tremendous enthusiasm). Daniel S. Dickinson represents someone, I suppose, in the state of New York; God knows he doesn't represent me. I can pledge you that our Daniel will stand cheek to jowl with your Daniel. (Cheers). He was never known to surrender slavery, but always to surrender liberty.

The bill of which you most justly complain, concerning the surrender of fugitive slaves, is to apply alike to your State and to our State, if it shall ever apply at all. but we have come here to make a common oath upon a common altar, that bill shall never take effect. (Applause). Honorable Senators may record their names in its behalf, and it may have the sanction of the House of Representatives; but we, the people, who are Superior to both Houses and the Executive, too (hear! hear!), we, the people, will never be human bipeds, to howl upon the track of the fugitive slave, even though led by the corrupt Daniel of your State, or the degraded one of ours. (Cheers).

Though there are many attempts to get up compromises--and there is no term which I detest more than this, it is always the term which makes right yield to wrong; it has always been accursed since Eve made the first compromise with the devil. (Repeated rounds of applause). I was saying, sir, that it is somewhat singular, and yet historically true, that when ever these compromises are proposed, there are men of the North who seem to foresee that Northern men, who think their constituency will not look into these matters, will seek to do more than the South demands. They seek to prove to Northern men that all is right and all is fair; and this is the game Webster is attempting to play.

"Oh," says Webster, "the will of God has fixed that matter, we will not re-enact the will of God." Sir, you remember the time in 1841, '42, '43 and '44, when it was said that Texas could never be annexed. The design of such dealing was that you should believe it, and then, when you thought yourselves secure, they would spring the trap upon you. And now it is their wish to seduce you into their belief that slavery never will go there, and then the slave holders will drive slavery there as fast as possible. I think that this is the most contemptible proposition of the whole, except the support of that bill which would attempt to make the whole North the slavecatchers of the South.

You will remember that the bill of Mr. Mason says nothing about color. Mr. Phillips, a man whom I always love (Applause), a man who taught me my horn-book on this subject of slavery, when I was a poor boy, has referred to Marshfield. There is a man who sometimes lives in Marshfield, and who has the reputation of having an honorable dark skin. Who knows that some postmaster may have to sit upon the very gentleman whose character you have been discussing tonight? (Hear! Hear!). "What is sauce for the goose is sauce for the gander." (Laughter). If this bill is to relieve grievances, why not make an application to the immortal Daniel of Marshfield? (Applause). There is no such thing as complexion mentioned. It is not only true that the colored man of Massachusetts--it is not only true that the fifty thousand colored men of New York may be taken--though I pledge you there is one, whose name is Sam Ward, who will never be taken alive! (Tremendous applause). Not only is it true that the fifty thousand black men in New York may be taken, but any one else also can be captured. My friend Theodore Parker alluded to Ellen Craft. I had the pleasure of taking tea with her, and accompanied her here to-night. She is far whiter than any who come here slave-catching. This line of distinction is so nice that you cannot tell who is white or black. As Alexander Pope used to say, "White and black soften and blend in so many thousand ways, that it is neither white nor black." (Loud plaudits).

This is the question, Whether a man (sic) a right to himself (sic) and his (sic) children, his hopes and his happiness, for this world and the world to come. That is a question which, according to this bill, may be decided by any backwoods postmaster in this State or any other. Oh, this is a monstrous proposition; and I do thank God that if the Slave Power has such demands to make on us, that the proposition has come now-now, that the people know what is being done-now that the public mind is turned toward this subject--now that they are trying to find out what is the truth on this subject!

Sir, what must be the moral influence of this speech of Mr. Webster on the minds of young men, lawyers and others, here in the North? They turn their eyes toward Daniel Webster as towards a superior mind, and a legal and constitutional oracle. If they shall catch the spirit of this speech, its influence upon them and upon following generations will be so deeply corrupting that it never can be wiped out or purged.

I am thankful that this, my first entrance into Boston, and my first introduction to Faneuil Hall, gives me the pleasure and privilege of uniting with you in uttering my humble voice against the two Daniel's, and of declaring, in behalf of our people, that if the fugitive slave is traced to our part of New York State, he (sic) shall have the law of Almighty God to protect him, the law which says, *"Thou shalt not return to the master the servant that has escaped unto thee, but he shall dwell with thee in thy gates, where it liketh him best."* And if our postmasters cannot maintain their constitutional oaths, and cannot live without playing the pander to the slave-hunter, they need not live at all. Such crises as these leave us to the right of Revolution, and if need be, that right we will, at whatever cost, most sacredly maintain.

Speech printed in *The Liberator* of April 5, 1850.

Selected Bibliography

SOURCES OF PRIMARY MATERIALS

American Antiquarian Society, Worcester, Massachusetts.

American Missionary Association Papers and Letters, Dillard University, New Orleans, Louisiana.

Annual Reports, Anti-Slavery Society of Canada (Toronto), 1852-1857.

Department of Rare Books and Special Collections, The University of Michigan, University Library, Ann Arbor, Michigan

Department of Regional History and Rare Books, University of Western Ontario, London 72, Canada.

Douglas Library Curator of Special Collections, Queens University at Kingston, Ontario, Canada.

Gerrit Smith Miller Papers, Syracuse University, Bird Library, Syracuse, New York.

Institute of Jamaica Archives, Kingston, Jamaica, West Indies.

Lincoln University of Missouri, University Library, Jefferson City, Missouri.

Onondaga Historical Society, Syracuse, New York

Samuel D. Porter Papers, University of Rochester Library, Rochester, New York.

University of Pennsylvania, University Library, Philadelphia, Pennsylvania.

William Lloyd Garrison Papers, Boston Public Library, Boston, Massachusetts.

REFERENCE WORKS

A Select List of Primary and Secondary Sources for the Study of the Negro Community in Canada from the Earliest Times to the Present Days, prepared by Sushil Kumar Jain, University of Saskatchewan Library, Regina, 1967.

Chase, Franklin R. *Syracuse and Its Environs: A History*. New York: Lewis Historical Publishing Co., 1924. 3 vols.

Cowles, George W., ed. *Landmarks of Wayne County*. Syracuse: D. Mason, 1895.

Dumond, Dwight Lowell. *A Bibliography of Antislavery in America*. Ann Arbor, Michigan, 1961.

Ellis, David M. et al. *A Short History of New York State*. Ithaca: New York: Cornell University Press, 1959.

Faibisoff, S.F. and A.S. Kelly. "A Bibliography of Newspapers in Fourteen New York State Counties." *New York History*. (1973): pp. 70-95.

Jones, Alexander, ed., *The Jerusalem Bible*. New York: Doubleday and Co., Inc., 1966.

Johnson, Allen ed., *Dictionary of American Biography*. New York: Charles Scribner's Sons, 1928.

Pride, Armistead Scott. *The Black Press: A Bibliography*. Jefferson City, Missouri: Prepared for The Association for Education in Journalism, Ad Hoc Committee on Minority Education, 1968.

Smith, H.P. *History of Cortland County*. Syracuse, New York: D. Mason and Co., 1895.

THESES AND DISSERTATIONS

Block, Muriel. "Beriah Green, The Reformer." Master's thesis., Syracuse University, 1935.

Britt, Joseph J. "The Gospel Ministry: The Oneida Institute and Rise of Abolitionism in the United States." Honors Program thesis. Boston College, 1970.

Burke, Ronald K. "Samuel Ringgold Ward: Christian Abolitionist." Ph.D. diss., Syracuse University, 1975.

Christian, H.N. "Samuel Cornish, Pioneer Negro Journalist." Master's thesis. Howard University, 1936.

Davis, E. Bradford. "Albert Barnes, 1798-1870: An Exponent of New School Presbyterianism." Th.D. diss., Princeton Theological Seminary, 1961.

Eggertsen, C.A. "The Monitorial System of Instruction in the United States," Ph.D. diss., University of Minnesota, 1939.

Ferrie, Walter L. "The New York Democracy: Division and Reunion, 1847-1852." Ph.D. diss., University of Pennsylvania, 1953.

Freeman, Rhoda G. "The Free Negro in New York City in the Era Before the Civil War." Ph.D. diss., Columbia University, 1966.

French, David Charles. "The Conversion of an American Radical: Elizur Wright, Jr. and the Abolitionist Committment." Ph.D. diss., Case Western Reserve University, 1970.

Fulkerson, Raymond Gerald, Frederick Douglass and the Anti-Slavery Crusade: His Career and Speeches, 1817-1861." Ph.D. diss., University of Illinois at Urbana-Champaign, 1971.

George, Carol. "Richard Allen and the Rise of the Independent Black Church Movement, 1788-1837." Ph.D. diss., Syracuse University, 1970 .

Henderson, Alice H. "The History of the New York State Antislavery Society." Ph.D. diss., University of Michigan, 1963.

Hendricks, John R. "History of the Liberty Party in New York State, 1838-1848." Ph.D. diss., Fordham University, 1958.

Howard, Victor B. "The Antislavery Movement in the Presbyterian Church, 1835-1861." Ph.D. diss., Ohio State University, 1961.

Jacobs, Donald Martin. "A History of the Boston Negro from the Revolution to the Civil War." Ph.D. diss., Boston University, 1968.

Johnson Clifton H. "The American Missionary Association, 1846-1861: A Study of Christian Abolitionism." Ph.D. diss., University of North Carolina, 1958.

Kennicott, Patrick C. "Negro Antislavery Speakers in America." Ph.D. diss., Florida State University, 1967.

Landon, Fred. "The Relation of Canada to the Anti-Slavery and Abolition Movements in the United States." Master's thesis, University of Western Ontario, 1919.

McKivigan, John R. "Abolitionism and the American Churches, 1830-1865: A Study of Attitudes and Tactics." Ph.D. diss., Ohio State University, 1974.

Moseberry, Lowell T. "An Historical Study of Negro Oratory in the United States to 1915." Ph.D. diss., University of Southern California, 1955.

Murray, Alexander L. "Canada and the Anglo-American Antislavery Movement: A Study in International Philanthropy." Ph.D. diss., University of Pennsylvania, 1960.

Pease, Jane H. "The Freshness of Fanaticism: Abby Kelly Foster: An Essay in Reform." Ph.D. diss., University of Rochester, 1969.

Serfman, Eli. "A History of the New York State Colonization Society." Ph.D. diss., New York University, 1965.

Simpson, Donald G. "Negroes in Ontario from Early Times to 1879." Ph.D. diss., University of Western Ontario, 1971.

Wander, Philip Charles. "The Image of the Negro in Three Movements: Abolitionism, Colonization, and Pro-Slavery." Ph.D. diss., University of Pittsburgh, 1968.

Warren, Claribel. "New York Central College." unpublished essay, Lamont Library, McGraw, New York, n.d.

Yanuck, Julius. The Fugitive Slave Law and the Constitution." Ph.D. diss., Columbia University, 1953.

NEWSPAPERS

The Aliened American, Cleveland, Ohio, 1851.

The Anglo-African Magazine, 1859.

The Anti-Slavery Record, 1835-1837.

The Colored American, 1840-1841.

The Cortland Standard. 1915, 1955.

The Daily Advertiser and Lawton's Commercial Gazette, Kingston, Jamaica, W.I. 1855-57.

The Falmouth Post and Jamaica General Advertiser, Kingston, Jamaica, W.I. 1855-1857.

The Hamilton Gazette, Ontario, Canada, 1851-1853.

The Impartial Citizen, Syracuse, Boston, 1849-1850.

The Liberator, Boston, 1839-1851.

The National Anti-Slavery Standard, 1840-1850.

The North Star, Rochester, New York, 1847-1851.

Frederick Douglass's Paper, Rochester, New York, 1851-1854.

The Syracuse Daily Standard, Syracuse, New York, 1851-1853.

The Provincial Freeman, Toronto, Chatham, Canada, 1853.
The Syracuse Reveille, Syracuse, New York, 1849.
The Toronto Examiner, 1852.
The Toronto Globe, 1851-1853.
The True American, Cortland, New York, 1845.
The Voice of the Fugitive, Sandwich, Windsor, Canada, 1851-1853.

PRINTED PRIMARY SOURCES

Abel, Annie H. and Frank J. Klingberg. *A Sidelight on Anglo-American Relations, 1839-1858*. Washington, D.C., 1927.

Andrews Charles C. *The History of the New York African Free-School Reprint*. New York: Negro Univeristy Press, 1969.

Aristotle. *Rhetoric and Poetics*. trans., W. Rhys Roberts and Ingram Bywater. New York: Random House, Inc., 1954.

Birney, James G. *The American Churches the Bulwarks of American Slavery*. Concord, New Hampshire, 1842; 1885.

Blassingame, John W. ed. *The Frederick Douglass Papers*. Ser. I, vols. 1, 2, and 3. New Haven: Yale University Press, 1979, 1982, 1985.

Brown, Henry Box. *Narrative of Henry Box Brown, Who Escaped Slavery In A Box 3 Feet Long and 2 Wide*. ed. Charles Stearns. Boston, 1848, 1849.

Cicero, Marcus Tullius. *The Rhetorica Ad Herrenium*. trans. Harry Caplan. Cambridge, Massachusetts: Harvard Univesity Press, 1954.

Crummell, Alexander. *Africa and America*. Springfield: Wiley & Co., 1891.

------. *The Greatness of Christ*. New York, 1882.

Delany, Martin R. *The Condition, Elevation, Emigration, and Destiny of the Colored People of the United States, Politically Considered*. Reprint. 1852. New York: Arno Press and the New York Times, 1969.

Douglass, Frederick. *Narration of the Life of Frederick Douglass*. Reprint. 1845. Boston: Signet Books, 1968.

------. *Life and Times of Frederick Douglass*. Reprint. 1845, London: Collier-Macmillan, 1962.

Garnet, Henry Highland. *Walker's Appeal, With A Brief Sketch of His Life*. New York, 1848.

Garrison, William Lloyd. *Thoughts on African Colonization.* Boston, 1832.

Garrison, W.P. and F.J. Garrison. *Life of William Lloyd Garrison*, 3 vols. New York. 1885-1889.

Loguen, Jermain W. *The Reverend Jermain Wesley Loguen as a Slave and as a Freeman.* New York. 1859.

May, Samuel J. *Some Recollections of Our Anti-Slavery Conflict.* Boston, 1869.

Penn, I. Garland. *The Afro-American Press and Its Editors.* Reprint. 1865. New York: Arno Press and the New York Times, 1969.

Pennington, James W.C. *The Fugitive Blacksmith.* London, 1849.

Ripley, Peter., ed. *The Black Abolitionist Papers.* 2 vols. Chapel Hill: University of North Carolina Press, 1985.

Still, William. *Underground Railroad.* Philadelphia, 1872.

Tocqueville, Alexis de. *Democracy in America.* Reprint. 1863. New York: Washington Square Press, 1964.

Ward, Samuel Ringgold. *Autobiography Of A Fugitive Negro.* Reprint. 1855. New York: The Arno Press, The New York Times, 1968.

------. *Autobiography Of A Fugitive Negro.* Reprint. 1855. Chicago: Johnson Publishing Co., Inc., 1970.

------. "Reflections Upon the Gordon Rebellion." (Jamaica, W.I. 1866).

Woodson, Carter G. *The Mind of the Negro As Reflected In Letters Written During the Crisis, 1800-1860.* Washington, D.C.: Associated Publishers, 1920.

------. *The History of the Negro Church.* Washington, D.C.: Associated Publishers, 1921.

------. *The Education of the Negro Prior to 1861.* Washington, D.C.:Associated Publishers, 1919.

Wright, Henry C. "My First Acquaintance With Garrison and Antislavery." *Liberty Bell.* Boston, 1846.

PRINTED SECONDARY SOURCES

Adams, James Truslow. "Disenfranchisement of Negroes in New England." *American Historical Review* 30, (1925): 546-547.

Allen, James E. "Samuel Ringgold Ward." *Negro History Bulletin* (1941): 41.

Aptheker, Herbert. *American Negro Slave Revolts*. New York: International Publishers, 1963.

------. "Militant Abolitionism." *Journal of Negro History* 26 (1941): 438-484.

------. "The Negro in the Abolitionist Movement." *Science and Society* 5 (1941): 2-23.

Auer, J. Jeffrey, ed. *Anti-Slavery and Disunion, 1858-1861: Studies in the Rhetoric of Compromise and Conflict*. New York: Harper & Row, 1963.

Baker, Houston A., Jr. *Black Literature in America*. New York: McGraw-Hill Book Co., 1973.

Barnes, Gilbert Hobbs. *The Antislavery Impulse*. New York: D. Appleton-Century Co., 1933.

Bartlett, Irving H. *Wendell Phillips: Brahman Radical*. Boston: Beacon Press, 1961.

Bell, Howard. "National Negro Conventions in the Middle 1840's." *Journal of Negro History* 42 (1957): 55-70.

------. "Free Negroes in the North, 1830-1835, A Study in National Cooperation." *The Journal of Negro Education* (1957): 447-455.

-----. "Some Reform Interests of the Negro During the 1850's As Reflected in State Conventions." *Phylon* (1960): 173-181.

------. "The American Moral Reform Society, 1836-1841." *The Journal of Negro Education* (1958): 34-40.

Bennett, Lerone. *Before the Mayflower: A History of the Negro in America, 1619-1966*. Chicago: Johnson Publishing Co., 1966.

Berwanger, Eugene M. "Negrophobia in Northern Proslavery and Antislavery Thought." *Phylon* (1972).

Billington, Ray Allen. "James Forten: Forgotten Abolitionist." *Negro History Bulletin* 13 (1949): 31-36, 75.

Blassingame, John W. ed. *Slave Testimony: Two Centuries of Letters, Speeches, Interviews, and Autobiographies*. Baton Rouge: Louisiana State University Press, 1977.

Blockett, R.J.M. "Fugitive Slaves in Britain: The Odyssey of William and Ellen Craft." *Journal of American Studies* 12 (1978): 41-64.

Boller, Paul F. "Washington, the Quakers and Slavery." *Journal of Negro History* 46 (1961): 83-88.

Brewer, W.M. "Henry Highland Garnet." *The Journal of Negro Education* (1928).

Bullock, Penelope. *The Afro-American Periodical Press, 1838-1909.* Baton Rouge: Louisiana State University Press, 1981.

Burke, Ronald K. "*The Impartial Citizen* of Samuel Ringgold Ward." *Journalism Quarterly* 49 (1972): 759-760.

Burns, Roger A. "A Quaker's Antislavery Crusade: Anthony Benezet." *Quaker History* 65 (1976): 81-92.

Butterfield, Herbert. *The Whig Interpretation of History.* New York: W.W. Norton, 1966.

Butterfield, Stephen. *Black Autobiography in America.* Amherst, MA: University of Massachusetts, 1974.

Campbell, Stanley W. *The Slave Catchers: Enforcement of the Fugitive Slave Law, 1850-1860.* Chapel Hill: University of North Carolina Press, 1970.

Champion, T.E. The Underground Railroad and One of Its Operators." *Canadian Magazine* (1895): 9-16.

Clayton, W.W. *History of Onondaga County.* Syracuse: D. Mason and Co., 1878.

Commager, Henry Steele. *The Era of Reform, 1830-1860.* Princeton, N.J.: Van Nostrand, 1960.

Cone, James H. *Black Theology and Black Power.* New York: The Seabury Press, 1969.

Conrad, Earl. *Harriet Tubman, Negro Soldier and Abolitionist.* New York: International Publishers, 5th printing, 1973.

Cooper, Frederick. "Elevating the Race: The Social Thought of Black Leaders, 1827-1850." *American Quarterly* (1972): 604-625.

Cooper, John J. "The Mission to the Fugitive Slave at London." *Ontario History* 46 (1954).

Cowles, George W. ed. *Landmarks of Wayne County.* Syracuse: D. Mason and Co., 1895.

Cross, Whitney R. *The Burned-Over District: The Social and Intellectual History of Enthusiastic Religion in Western New York, 1800-1850.* New York: Harper & Row, 1965.

Dann, Martin E. *The Black Press, 1827-1890: The Quest for National Identity.* New York: Putnam, 1971.

Davis, David Brion. *The Problem of Slavery in Western Culture.* Ithaca: Cornell University Press, 1966.

Detweiler, Frederick G. *The Negro Press in the United States.* Chicago: University of Chicago Press, 1922.

Dick, Robert C. *Black Protest: Issues & Tactics.* Westport, Connecticut: Greenwood Press, 1974.

Dillon, Merton L. *Elijah P. Lovejoy: Abolitionist Editor.* Urbana: University of Illinois Press, 1961.

------. *The Abolitionists: The Growth of A Dissenting Minority.* DeKalb: Northern Illinois University Press, 1974.

Drew, Benjamin. *The Refugee: A Northside View of Slavery.* Introd. by T.G. Edelstein. Reading, Massachusetts: Addison-Wesley Publ., 1969.

Duberman, Martin B. ed. *The Antislavery Vanguard: New Essays on the Abolitionists.* Princeton: Princeton University Press, 1965.

Dumond, Dwight Lowell. *Antislavery: The Crusade for Freedom in America.* New York: W.W. Norton & Co., 1961.

Eaton, Clement. *The Mind of the South* Louisiana State University Press, 1967.

Elkins, Stanley M. *Slavery: A Problem in American Institutional and Intellectual Life.* New York: Grosset & Dunlap, 1963.

Faibisoff, Sylvia G. and Abigail S. Kelly. "Bibliography of Newspapers in Fourteen New York State Counties." *New York History* (1973).

Field, Phyllis F. *The Politics of Race in New York: The Struggle for Black Suffrage in the Civil War Era.* Ithaca: Cornell University Press, 1982.

Filler, Lewis. *The Crusade Against Slavery, 1830-1860.* New York: Harper & Row Publ., 1960.

Fladeland, Betty L. "Who Were the Abolitionists?" *Journal of Negro History* 49 (1964): 99-115.

Foner, Eric. "Politics and Prejudice: the Free-Soil Party and the Negro, 1849-1853." *Journal of Negro History* 50 (1965): 239-256.

Foner, Philip S., ed. *The Life and Writings of Frederick Douglass.* 4 vols. New York: International Publ., 1950, 1952, 1955.

Fox, Dixon Ryan. "The Negro Vote in Old New York." *Political Science Quarterly* 32 (1917): 252-275.

Fox, Early Lee. *American Colonization Society, 1817-1840.* Baltimore: Johns Hopkins University Press, 1919.

Frazier, E. Franklin. *The Negro Church in America.* New York: Schocken Books, 1968.

Gara, Larry. "The Professional Fugitives in the Abolition Movement." *Wisconsin Magazine of History* 48 (1965): 196-204.

------. "Some Self-Help Plans of Fugitive Slaves." *Negro History Bulletin* (1952).

Gates, Henry Louis Jr. ed. *Black Literature and Literary Theory.* New York: Metheun, Inc., 1984.

Gibson, Donald B. ed. *Afro-American Literary Studies in the 1990's.* Chicago: The University of Chicago Press, 1989.

Griffin, Clifford S. "The Abolitionists and the Benevolent Scieties, 1831-1861." *Journal of Negro History* 44 (1959): 195-216.

Gross, Bella, "Freedom's Journal and the Rights of All." *Journal of Negro History* 17 (1932).

Harlow, Ralph V. *Gerrit Smith, Philanthropist and Reformer.* New York: Henry Holt & Co., 1939.

Hart, Albert Bushnell. *Slavery and Abolition, 1831-1841.* New York: Harper & Bros., 1906.

Harwood, Thomas F. "British Evangelical Abolitionism and American Churches in the 1830's." *Journal of Southern History* 28 (1962): 287-306.

Higginson, Thomas Wentworth. "The American Lecture System." *Macmillan's Magazine* 18 (1868): 55.

Hirsch, Leo. "New York and the Negro from 1783-1865." *Journal of Negro History* 16 (1931): 415-487.

Holland, Frederick May. *Frederick Douglass, The Colored Orator.* New York: Funk & Wagnalls Co., 1891.

Hume, John F. *The Abolitionists, Together With Personal Memories of the Struggle for Human Rights*, 1830-1864. New York: Knopf, 1961.

Kerber, Linda K. "Abolitionists and Amalgamators: The New York City Race Riots of 1834." *New York History* 48 (1967): 28-39.

Klingberg, Frank J. *The Antislavery Movement in England.* New Haven: Yale University Press, 1926.

Kraditor, Aileen. *Means and Ends in American Abolitionism.* New York: Pantheon Press, 1968.

Kyles, L.W. "The Contribution of the Negro to the Religious Life Of America." *Journal of Negro History* 11 (1926).

Lader, Lawrence. *The Bold Brahmins: New England's War Against Slavery, 1831-1863.* New York: E.P. Dutton & Co., Inc., 1961.

Landon, Fred. "Abolitionist Interest in Upper Canada." *Ontario History* 44 (1925): 155-172.

------. "The Antislavery Society of Canada." *Journal of Negro History* 4 (1919): 33-40.

------. "The Buxton Settlement in Canada." *Journal of Negro History* 3 (1918): 366-367.

------. "Henry Bibb: A Colonizer." *Journal of Negro History* 5 (1920): 437-447.

------. "The Negro Migration to Canada After the Passing of the Fugitive Slave Act." *Journal of Negro History* 5 (1920): 22-27. .

------. "Samuel Ringgold Ward." In *Dictionary of American Biography* 19, ed. Allen Johnson. New York: D. Appleton & Co., 1936.

Litwack, Leon F. *North of Slavery, The Negro in the Free State, 1790-1860*. Chicago: University of Chicago Press, 1931.

------. "The Abolition Dilemma: The Antislavery Movement and the Northern Negro." *New England Quarterly* (1961): 50-73.

Loggins, Vernon. *The Negro Author, His Development in America.* New York: Columbia University Press, 1931.

Loveland, Anne C. "Evangelicalism and Immediate Emancipation in American Antislavery Thought." *The Journal of Southern History* (1966).

Martyn, Carlos. *Wendell Phillips: The Agitator*. New York: Funk & Wagnalls Co., 1890.

Mathews, Donald G. *Agitation for Freedom: The Abolitionist Movement*. New York: John Wiley & Sons, Inc., 1972.

Mathieson, William Law. *British Slavery and Its Abolition, 1823-1838*. London: Longmans, Green & Co., 1926.

Mays, Benjamin E. "The American Negro and the Christian Religion." *Journal of Negro Education* (1939): 53-58.

McCormac, E.I. "White Servitude in Maryland, 1634-1820." *Johns Hopkins University Studies in Historical and Political Science* (1904).

McCormick, Richard P. "William Whipper: Moral Reformer." *Pennsylvania History* 43 (1975): 23-48.

Meier, August and Elliot Rudwick, eds. *The Making of Black America*. vol. 1 New York: Atheneum, 1969.

Merrill, Walter M. *Against the Wind and Tide: A Biography of William Lloyd Garrison*. Cambridge, MA: Harvard University Press, 1963.

Murray, Alexander. "*The Provincial Freeman*: A New Source for the History of the Negro in Canada and the United States." *Journal of Negro History* 43 (1959).

Ofari, Earl. *'Let Your Motto Be Resistance': The Life and Thought of Henry Highland Garnet*. Boston: Beacon Press, 1972.

O'Kelly, Charlotte G. "Black Newspapers and the Black Protest Movement: Their Historical Relationship, 1827-1945." *Phylon* 43 (1982): 1-14.

Osofsky, Gilbert. "Abolitionists, Irish Immigrants, and the Dilemma of Romantic Nationalism." *American Historical Review* 80 (1975): 889-912.

Pease, William H. and Jane H. *Black Utopia: Negro Communal Experiments in America*. Madison, Wisconsin, 1963.

------. eds. *The Antislavery Argument*. New York: Bobbs-Merrill Co., 1965.

Perry, Lewis. *Radical Abolitionism: Anarchism and the Government of God in Antislavery Thought*. Ithaca, N.Y.: Cornell Univeristy Press, 1973.

Porter, Dorothy P. "The Organized Educational Activities of Negro Literary Societies, 1828-1846." *Journal of Negro Education* 20 (1936): 557-577.

Quarles, Benjamin. *Black Abolitionists*. New York: Oxford University Press, 1969.

------. *The Negroes in the Making of America*. New York: Collier Books, 1964.

------. "Letters From Negro Leaders to Gerrit Smith." *Journal of Negro History* 36 (1942).

Riach, Douglas C. "Daniel O'Connell and American Slavery." *Irish Historical Studies* 20 (1976): 3-25.

Rice, C. Duncan. "The Antislavery Mission of George Thompson to the United States, 1834-1835. *Journal of American Studies* 29 (1968): 13-31.

Richards, Leonard L. *'Gentlemen of Property and Standing,' Anti-Abolition Mobs in Jacksonian America*. New York: Oxford University Press, 1970.

Riddell, William Renwich. "Further Notes on the Slave in Canada." *Journal of Negro History* 9 (1924).

------. "Slavery in Canada." *Journal of Negro History* 5 (1920).

------. "The Slave in Upper Canada." *Journal of Negro History* 4 (1919).

------. "The Slave in New York." Journal of Negro History 13 (1928).

Robertson, Constance (Noyes). *Fire Bell in the Night*. New York: H.H. Holt and Co., 1944.

Rohman, D. *Here's Whitesboro: An Informal History*. New York: Stratford House, 1949.

Ruchames, Louis. *The Abolitionists: A Collection of Their Writings*. New York: G.P. Putnam's Sons, 1963.

Ruchkin, Judith P. "The Abolition of Colored Schools in Rochester, New York: 1832-1856." *New York History* 51 (1970): 377-393.

Russell, Robert R. "What Was the Compromise of 1850?" *Journal of Southern History* (1956): 293-309.

Scruggs, Otey M. "Alexander Crummell (1819-1898), Pioneer, Black, Intellectual, Cultural Materialist, and Founder of St. Luke's Church." Paper read before Black Episcopaleans of Washington, D.C. (March, 1974).

Sevitch, Benjamin. "The Well-Planned Riot of October 21, 1835: Utica's Answer to Abolitionism." *New York History* 50 (1969): 251-263.

Shapiro, Samuel. "The Rendition of Anthony Burns." *Journal of Negro History* 44 (1959): 34-51.

Sherwin, Oscar. *Prophet of Liberty: The Life and Times of Wendell Phillips*. New York: Bookman Associates, 1956.

Sherwood, Henry Noble. "The Formation of the American Colonization Society." *Journal of Negro History*. 2 (1917): 209-228.

Silverman, Jason H. "The American Fugitive Slave in Canada: Myths and Realities." *Southern Studies* 19 (1980): 215-227.

Smith, Theodore Clarke. *The Liberty and Free Soil Parties in the Northwest*. New York: Russell & Russell, 1967.

Smith, Timothy L. *Revivalism and Social Reform*. New York: Harper & Row, 1957.

Sorin, Gerald. *The New York Abolitionists: A Case Study of Political Radicalism*. Westport, Connecticut: Greenwood Publishing Corp., 1971.

Sperry, Earl E. *The Jerry Rescue*. Syracuse, New York: Onondaga Historical Association, 1924.

Stampp, Kenneth M. *The Peculiar Institution: Slavery in the Ante-Bellum South*. New York: Random House, 1956.

Staudenraus, P.J. *The African Colonization Movement, 1816-1865*. New York: Columbia Univeristy Press, 1962.

Stewart, James B. "The Aims and Impact of Garrisonian Abolitionism, 1840-1860." *Civil War History* 15 (1969): 197-209.

Strother, Horatio T. *The Underground Railroad in Connecticut*. Middletown, Connecticut: Wesleyan University Press, 1962.

Stuckey, Sterling. "Through the Prism of Folklore: The Black Ethos in Slavery." *Massachusetts Review* (1968).

Sydnor, Charles S. "Pursuing Fugitive Slaves." *The South Atlantic Quarterly* (1929): 152-164.

Tanner, Edwin Platt. "Gerrit Smith, An Interpretation." New York *Historical Society Quarterly* 5 (1924): 21-39.

Temperley, Howard. *British Antislavery, 1833-1870*. Columbia, S.C.: University of South Carolina Press, 1972.

Tyler, Alice Felt. *Freedom's Ferment: Phases of American Social History From the Colonial Period to the Outbreak of the Civil War*. New York: Harper & Row, 1962.

Ullman, Victor. *Martin R. Delany: The Beginnings of Black Nationalism*. Boston: Beacon Press, 1971.

Wallace, Les. "Charles Lenox Remond: The Last Prince of Abolitionism." *Negro History Bulletin* 40 (1977): 696-701.

Wander, Philip C. "Salvation Through Separation: The Image of the Negro in the American Colonization Society." *The Quarterly Journal of Speech* 57 (1971): 57-67.

Warner, Robert Austin. *New Haven Negroes: A Social History*. New Haven: Yale University Press, 1940.

------. "Amos Gerry Beman, 1812-1874.: A Memoir On a Forgotten Leader." *Journal of Negro History* 22 (1937): 200-221.

Weinstein, Allen and Frank Otto Gatell. *American Negro Slavery: A Modern Reader*. New York: Oxford University Press, 1968.

Weisberger, Bernard A. *They Gathered at the River: The Story of the Great Revivalists* Boston: Little, Brown & Co., 1958.

Wesley, Charles. *Richard Allen, Apostle of Freedom*. Washington: Assocaited Publishers, Inc., 1935.

------. "Negro Suffrage in the Period of Constitution-Making, 1787-1865." *Journal of Negro History* 32 (1947): 154-160.

------. "The Negro in the Organization of Abolition." *Phylon* 2 (1941): 223-235.

------. "The Participation of Negroes in Antislavery Political Parties." *Journal of Negro History* 29 (1944): 32-74.

Winks, Robin W. *The Blacks in Canada*. New Haven: Yale University Press, 1971.

Wolseley, Roland E. *The Black Press, U.S.A.* 2d ed. Ames, Iowa: The Iowa State University Press, 1990.

Woodson, Carter G. *Negro Orators and Their Orations*. New York: Russell & Russell, 1969.

Work, Monroe N. "The Life of Charles B. Ray." *Journal of Negro History* 4 (1919).

Wyatt-Brown, Bertram. *Lewis Tappan & The Evangelical War Against Slavery*. Cleveland, Ohio: Case Western Reserve University Press, 1965.

Zinn, Howard. *SNCC: The New Abolitionists*. Boston: Beacon Press, 1965.

BOOKS AND ARTICLES OF SPEECH STUDIES AND RHETORICAL CRITICISM

Aly, Bower, *The Rhetoric of Alexander Hamilton*. New York: Columbia University Press, 1941.

Andrews, James R. "The Rhetoric of Coercion and Persuasion: The Reform Bill of 1832." *The Quarterly Journal of Speech* 56, no. 2 (1970): 187-195

------. "Reflections of the National Character in American Rhetoric." *The Quarterly Journal of Speech* 57, no. 2 (1971): 316-324.

------. "Disintegration and Liberation in Rhetorical Studies." *Today's Speech* 20, no. 3 (1972): 39-44.

------. *A Choice of Worlds: The Practice and Criticism of Public Discourse*. New York: Harper & Row, 1973.

Aristotle. *The Rhetoric of Aristotle*. Lane Cooper, trans. Englewood Cliffs, N.J.: Prentice-Hall, Inc., 1960.

Arnold, Carroll. *Criticism of Oral Rhetoric*. Columbus, OH: Charles Merrill, 1974.

Asante, Molefi K. and Deborah F. Atwater. "The Rhetorical Condition as Symbolic Structure in Discourse." *Communication Quarterly* 34 (1986): 170-177.

Asante, Molefi K. "A Metatheory for Black Communication." *The Journal of Black Psychology* 1 (1975): 30-41.

Auer, J. Jeffrey, ed. *Antislavery and Disunion, 1858-1861. Studies in the Rhetoric of Compromise and Conflict.* New York and Evanston: Harper & Row, 1963.

Backes, James G. "Rhetorical Criticism: Yet Another Emphasis." *Western Speech* 26 (1962): 164-167.

Baird, A Craig and Lester Thonssen. *Speech Criticism.* New York: The Ronald Press, 1948.

------. "The Study of Speeches." *American Public Address, 1740-1952.* New York: McGraw-Hill, 1956.

Bashford, Bruce. "The Rhetorical Method in Literary Criticism." *Philosophy and Rhetoric* 9 (1976): 133-146.

Baskerville, Barnet. "Principal Themes of Nineteenth Century Critics of Oratory." *Speech Monographs* 19 (1952): 11-26.

------. "The Critical Method in Speech." Central States Speech Journal 4 (1953): 1-5.

------. "Must We All Be Rhetorical Critics?" *The Quarterly Journal of Speech* 63 (1977): 107-116.

------. *The People's Voice: The Orator in American Society.* Lexington: The University Press of Kentucky, 1979.

Bass, Jeff D. and Richard Cherwitz. "Imperial Mission and Manifest Destiny: A Case Study of Political Myth in Rhetorical Discourse." *The Southern Speech Communication Journal* 43 (1978): 213-232

Beale, Walter H. "On the Classification of Discourse Performances." *Rhetoric Society Quarterly* 7 (1977): 31-40.

Benson, Thomas W. "Rhetoric and Autobiography: The Case of Malcolm X." *The Quarterly Journal of Speech* 60 (1974): 1-13.

Berlin, James A. "The Transformation of Invention in Nineteenth Century American Rhetoric." *The Southern Speech Communication Journal* 46 (1981): 292-304.

Bitzer, Lloyd. "The Rhetorical Situation." *Philosophy and Rhetoric* 1 (1968): 1-14.

Black, Edwin. *Rhetorical Criticism: A Study in Method.* New York: Macmillan, 1965.

------. "The Second Persona." *The Quarterly Journal of Speech* 56 (1970): 109-119.

Bormann, Ernest G. "Fantasy and Rhetorical Vision: The Rhetorical Criticism of Social Reality." *The Quarterly Journal of Speech* 58 (1972): 396-407.

------. *Forerunners of Black Power: The Rhetoric of Abolition.* Englewood Cliffs, N.J.: Prentice-Hall, 1971.

Brockriede, Wayne. "Dimensions of the Concept of Rhetoric." *The Quarterly Journal of Speech* 54 (1968): 1-12.

Browne, Stephen H. "Daniel O'Connell and the Language of Confrontation." *The Southern Speech Communication Journal* 48 (1983): 65-76.

Burke, Kenneth. *A Rhetoric of Motives.* Englewood Cliffs, N.Y.: Prentice-Hall, 1950.

Campbell, Karlyn Kohrs. "The Rhetoric of Radical Black Nationalism: A Case Study in Self-Conscious Criticism." *Central States Speech Journal* 22 (1971): 151-160.

------. "Style and Content in the Rhetoric of Early Afro-American Feminists." *The Quarterly Journal of Speech* 72 (1986): 434-445.

------. *The Rhetorical Act.* Belmont, California: Wadsworth Publ., 1982.

Clark, E. Culpepper and Raymie E. McKerrow. "The Historiographical Dilemma of Myrdal's American Creed: Rhetoric's Role in Rescuing a Historical Moment." *The Quarterly Journal of Speech* 73 (1987): 303-316.

Conley, Thomas. "Ancient Rhetoric and Modern Genre Criticism." *Communication Quarterly* 29 (1979): 53.

Diffley, Kathleen. "'Erecting Anew The Standard Of Freedom': Salmon P. Chase's 'Appeal of the Independent Democrats' and the Rise of the Republican Party." *The Quarterly Journal of Speech* 74 (1988): 401-415

Edelman, Murray. "The Language of Participation and the Language of Resistance." *Human Communication Research* 3 (1977): 160-169.

Erickson, Keith V. "Black Messiah: The Father Divine Peace Mission Movement." *The Quarterly Journal of Speech* 63 (1977): 428-438.

Farrell, Thomas B. "Knowledge, Consensus and Rhetorical Theory." *The Quarterly Journal of Speech* 62 (1976): 1-14.

Fisher, Walter R. "Method in Rhetorical Criticism." *The Southern Speech Communication Journal* 35 (1969): 101-109.

Gold, Ellen Reid. "The Grimke Sisters and the Emergence of the Woman's Rights Movement." *The Southern Speech Communication Journal* 46 (1981): 341-360.

Grassi, Ernesto. *Rhetoric As Philosophy.* University Park: Pennsylvania State University Press, 1980.

Gregg, Richard B. "The Ego Function of the Rhetoric of Protest." *Philosophy and Rhetoric* 4 (1971): 71-91.

Griffin, Leland M. "The Rhetoric of Historical Movements." *The Quarterly Journal of Speech* 38 (1952): 183-188.

Haiman, Franklyn S. "Nonverbal Communication and the First Amendment: The Rhetoric of the Streets Revisited." *The Quarterly Journal of Speech* 68 (1982): 371-383.

Hammerback, John C. "The Rhetoric of A Righteous Reform: George Washington Julian's 1852 Campaign Against Slavery." *Central States Speech Journal.* 22 (1971): 85-93.

Heath, Robert L. "Dialectical Confrontation: A Strategy of Black Radicalism." *Central States Speech Journal* 24 (1973): 168-177.

Holland, De Witte, ed. *Preaching in American History.* Nashville, Tennessee: Abingdon Press, 1969.

Johannesen, Richard L. "The Jeremiad and Jenkin Lloyd Jones." *Communication Monographs* 52 (1985): 156-172.

Johnstone, Christopher L. "Thoreau and Civil Disobedience: A Rhetorical Paradox." *The Quarterly Journal of Speech* 60 (1974): 313-322.

Kennicott, Patrick C. "Black Persuaders in the Antislavery Movement." *Speech Monographs* 27 (1970): 15-24.

King, Andrew A. "The Rhetorical Legacy of the Black Church." *Central States Speech Journal* 22 (1971): 179-185.

Logue, Cal M. "Transcending Coercion: The Communicative Strategies of Black Slaves on Antebellum Plantations." *The Quarterly Journal of Speech* 67 (1981): 31-46.

Martin, Howard. "The Fourth of July Oratory." *The Quarterly Journal of Speech* 54 (1958): 393-401.

Murphy, James J. *A Synoptic History of Classical Rhetoric.* Davis, California: Hermagoras Press, 1983.

Oravec, Christine. "Where Theory and Criticism Meet: A Look At Contemporary Rhetorical Theory." *Western Journal of Speech Communication* 46 (1982): 56-71.

Reed, Robert Michael. "The Case of Missionary Smith: A Crucial Incident in the Rhetoric of the British Antislavery Movement." *Central States Speech Journal*. 29 (1978): 61-71.

Ryan, Halford Ross and Bernard K. Duffy. *American Orators Before 1900: Critical Studies and Sources*. Westport Connecticut: Greenwood Press, 1987.

Scott, Robert L. and Donald K. Smith. "The Rhetoric of Confrontation." *The Quarterly Journal of Speech* 55 (1969): 1-8.

Smith, Arthur L. "Henry Highland Garnet: Black Revolutionary in Sheep's Vestments." *Central States Speech Journal* 21 (1970): 93-98.

------. *The Rhetoric of Black Revolution*. Boston: Allyn & Bacon, Inc., 1969.

Smith, Arthur L. and Stephen Robb. *The Voice of Black Rhetoric*. Boston: Allyn and Bacon, 1971.

Thomas, Gordon L. "John Brown's Courtroom Speech." *The Quarterly Journal of Speech* 48 (1962): 291-296.

Toulmin, Stephen. *The Uses of Argument*. Cambridge, England: Cambridge University Press, 1958.

Wander, Philip C. "The Savage Child: The Image of the Negro in the Pro-Slavery Movement." *Southern Speech Journal* 37 (1972): 335-360.

Weaver, Richard M. *The Ethics of Rhetoric*. Chicago: Henry Regnery Co., 1965.

Windt, Theodore O. "The Diatribe: Last Resort for Protest." *The Quarterly Journal of Speech* 58 (1972): 1-14.

Wrage, Ernest J. "The Ideal Critic." *Central States Speech Journal* 8 (1957): 20-23.

------. "Public Address: A Study in Social and Intellectual History." *The Quarterly Journal of Speech* 33 (1947): 451-457.

Index